£7.99

Rosemary Clark.

The Holy Spirit and Israel

Bruce D. Reekie

GW00401640

Sovereign World

Sovereign World Ltd
PO Box 777
Tonbridge
Kent TN11 9XT
England

ISBN: 1 85240 137 0

Typeset by CRB (Drayton) Typesetting Services, Drayton, Norwich
Printed in England by Clays Ltd, St Ives plc.

Contents

Foreword

It gives me genuine pleasure to commend this excellent book. Bruce Reekie has capably tackled an extremely important subject which surely needs to be clearly understood at this critical time in world history. Christians particularly need to grasp the significance of God's prophetic purposes for Israel. This tiny nation is centre stage for the dramatic introduction of Messiah's Kingdom rule.

The Holy Spirit and Israel deals with many relevant areas of truth in a very clear, concise and convincing manner. It is a very readable, yet serious perception of a very important subject.

I am truly delighted that this Australian author has presented us with this worthwhile book. I sincerely trust that it will achieve the wide readership it deserves and I pray that it will enrich and inspire every reader as it has myself.

Gerald Rowlands (Rev.)
Queensland
Australia

Author's Preface

Readers will note that *The Holy Spirit and Israel* does not deal at length with the much vaunted 'Palestinian Problem' – the tragic saga of Palestinian Arabs, made homeless (voluntarily and involuntarily) by the 1948 War of Independence.

Since June 1967, 'the Palestinians' have been mercilessly exploited by ruthless Arab leaders as part of a strategy to ostracize Israel from the international community. The quest for a 'two-state solution' is, as stated in the Palestinian Covenant, an incremental step in the acquisition of the whole Land and the destruction of the Jewish people.

Israel, for its part, has been guilty of some human rights violations in the course of this long running battle. However, it must be stated that no other nation, similarly placed, has demonstrated such patience and restraint as has Israel with the Palestinian Arabs.

The Holy Spirit and Israel is not designed to be a comprehensive treatise on the Middle East and its multitudinous problems. The spiritual mandate of this book is to provide a prophetic perspective on God's end-time purpose for Israel, and in particular, the long awaited outpouring of the Holy Spirit upon the House of David and the inhabitants of Jerusalem.

May it be duly used of God to inspire Christians to believe and pray!

Chapter 1

Loving Jerusalem

'If I forget you, O Jerusalem, let my right hand forget her skill! If I do not remember you, let my tongue cling to the roof of my mouth – If I do not exalt Jerusalem above my chief joy.'
(Psalm 137:5, 6)

Like a glittering diamond on a couch of velvet, the city of Jerusalem is set among the hills of Judea, in the geographical centre of the earth.

The destiny of all mankind is bound up in the life of this unique city.

Since the time of Abraham, Eretz Israel has been the principal theatre of world redemption. Upon this Divinely appointed stage, the unfolding drama of God's Kingdom Purpose is being played out before the eyes of men and angels.

The prophetic past, the prophetic present, and the prophetic future meet together in Israel. For Bible-believing Christians, Jerusalem and Israel constitute more than nostalgic memories of childhood Sunday School lessons.

For those with eyes to see and ears to hear, Israel pulsates with the Promise of Redemption. The Land is alive with the Breath of Life. The withered fig tree has again burst forth into fruitfulness, indicating that 'summer' – the consummation of God's redemptive purposes – is at hand! (Luke 21:29–33).

In the words of one evangelist:

'Each time I step upon the soil of Israel there is a feeling akin to awe that sweeps over me. My entire being seems to vibrate with the presence of God. Viewing the people as they plant and rebuild the Land makes me realize that I am at grips with a miracle. I see, hear and feel the mighty works that God is accomplishing in that tiny Land on the edge of man's wilderness.'[1]

As one perceives the uniqueness of the Land and the People of Israel from the perspective of the Word of God, one begins to understand the battle that is raging over the status of Jerusalem, the immigration of Russian Jews, the resettlement of Judea and Samaria, and the very principle of Israel's continued existence.

The hireling-prophet Balaam called Israel *'a people who dwell alone, not reckoning itself among the nations'* (Numbers 23:9). Thus, from the beginning of her existence Israel has been set apart from the nations, locked up unto a unique and awesome destiny. That uniqueness is no less apparent today, as Israel fights for survival in the midst of an increasingly hostile world.

Why does Israel regularly command the attention of the world's Press? What causes a tiny nation of five million people, occupying less than 1% of the earth's surface, to be such a major stumbling block in international affairs? Why is Jerusalem the most sought after and fiercely contested piece of real estate in the world?

To answer these questions, let us consider the **one thing** that sets Jerusalem and Israel apart from the rest of the world:

My Land, My City

The earth is the Lord's and all its fullness, the world and those who dwell therein (Psalm 24:1). However, God lays special claim to Israel in general, calling it *'My Land'*, and to Jerusalem in particular, calling it *'My City'*.

In the estimation of man, Jerusalem may not qualify as the biggest, the brightest or the best city in the world. She lacks some of the illustrious features and delectable attractions of other famous and fashionable centres.

Yet 'Jerusalem of Gold' possesses a splendour and a glory that is unparalleled among the cities of the world. Her adornment is more spiritual than physical; her attractiveness more heavenly than earthly.

The uniqueness of Jerusalem stems from the fact that God has chosen this city, and this city alone, to be the capital of His Kingdom.

What was foreshadowed in the reign of King David will be consummated in the reign of David's Greater Son, *Yeshua HaMashiach*.

From His Throne in Jerusalem, the Lord Jesus will rule over the nations, and from the nations people will come up to Jerusalem to worship the King. The whole earth will be filled with the knowledge of the glory of the Lord, and that glory will emanate from Messiah's Throne in Jerusalem!

Jerusalem, therefore, has a hope of redemption and glory that is without peer; a destiny unrivalled by that of any other metropolis, whether great or small, rich or poor, famous or obscure.

Natural and Spiritual Elevation

Jerusalem is one of the highest points in Eretz Israel. It is situated on the summit of three hills at an elevation of 2,550 feet above sea level. From whatever direction one approaches Jerusalem, one must 'ascend' to the City. For this reason, one always speaks of 'going up to Jerusalem' or in Hebrew, *'la'alot l'Yerushalayim'*.

However, Jerusalem's 'elevation' primarily has to do with her identity and destiny as the City of God. Of all the cities in the world, only Jerusalem is referred to as:

The Holy City	(Isaiah 52:1)
The City of the Great King	(Matthew 5:35)
The Throne of the Lord	(Jeremiah 3:17)
The Place of God's Name	(2 Chronicles 33:4)
The Object of God's Love	(Psalm 87:1–3)

The Cause of God's Joy	(Isaiah 65:19)
The Dwelling Place of God	(Psalm 135:21)
The Seat of God's Government	(Isaiah 2:3)
A Crown of Glory and a Royal Diadem	(Isaiah 62:3)
The City of Truth	(Zechariah 8:3)

In this sense, Jerusalem is the most 'elevated' city on the face of the earth!

Jerusalem of today may be, at best, a dim reflection and at worst, a contradiction of its God-given designation. But people of faith can see, through the eye of the Spirit, the restoration of all things that the prophets have spoken. This process of restoration will be completed in the Day of our Lord's appearing.

Loving What God Loves

The *Shema*, the Great Commandment and Confession of Faith, enjoins us to *'love the Lord our God with all our heart, with all our soul, and with all our strength'* (Deuteronomy 6:5).

'Loving God' presupposes conformity to His image and unanimity with His purpose. To fear the Lord is to hate evil (Proverbs 8:13). To love God is to choose that which pleases Him (Isaiah 56:4), to rejoice in that which He creates (Isaiah 65:18), and to delight in that which He establishes (Isaiah 58:13). Simply put, it is loving that which God loves!

God's attitude toward Mount Zion and Jerusalem is clearly expressed by the sons of Korah in Psalm 87:1–2;

> *'His foundation is in the holy mountains. The LORD loves the gates of Zion more than all the dwellings of Jacob. Glorious things are spoken of you, O city of God! Selah.'*

Should we who love God, lightly esteem that which is precious in His sight?

'But,' some would say, *'We, like Abraham, are looking for a city with eternal foundations, whose builder and maker is God'* (Hebrews 11:10). *'Our citizenship is in Heaven'* (Philippians

3:20). *'We have come to the heavenly Mount Zion, the eternal city of the Living God, the New Jerusalem'* (Hebrews 12:22). *'It is the Jerusalem above that is the mother of us all'* (Galatians 4:26).

Well said! I could do nothing but agree with that which is so clearly stated in the Word of God.

However, does that mean that God is finished with natural Jerusalem? Does that mean that His eyes are no longer on this ancient city, that He no longer has a place for her in His economy, that she has been discarded and consigned to a fate like that of ancient Nineveh or Ur?

NO! A thousand times, NO! The Prophetic Word makes it clear that God has unfinished business in Jerusalem, and that consequently, it will become increasingly prominent as this age draws to a close, and indeed, will occupy a unique place in the age to come!

The Lord Jesus acknowledged that under the New Covenant, true spiritual worship would no longer be restricted to a geographical location like Jerusalem, and the Presence of God would no longer reside in a physical building like the temple (John 4:21–24).

However, Jesus warned against swearing by Jerusalem, *'for it is the city of the Great King'* (Matthew 5:35). Notice that Jesus didn't say, 'It *was* the city of the Great King', but rather, *'it is the city of the Great King'*. God has a claim to this city which transcends the passage of time and the changing face of world politics!

Moreover, Jesus declared that *'Jerusalem will be trampled by Gentiles until the times of the Gentiles are fulfilled'* (Luke 21:24). Notice once again that Jesus didn't say, 'Jerusalem will be trampled by Gentiles, *period*', but rather, *'Jerusalem will be trampled by Gentiles until ...'*

In other words, Jerusalem will be temporarily set aside and subjected to Gentile domination, but in the end will be restored to a place of glory and honour among the nations.

And it is to the Mount of Olives, in the environs of a restored Jerusalem, that Jesus will one day return as King of Kings and Lord of Lords, and it is from this City that He will rule over all the earth! (Zechariah 14:4, 9)

Thus, the restored city of Jerusalem is an umbilical cord that connects the present age of humanistic rebellion with the 'new age' of Messianic government.

Present-day Jerusalem is, in spite of her imperfections, a link with the Jerusalem that is to come, which is the hope of us all.

How should we respond to the unfailing love of God for His Land and His City? The answer is found in the very same Psalm:

> *'The singers as well as the players on instruments shall say, All my springs (my sources of life and joy) are in you (city of our God).'* (Psalm 87:7, Amplified)

Let us join in saying to Jerusalem: 'You are to us a source of life and joy!'

May They Prosper Who Love You

This very century, God has arisen and shown mercy to Zion. Why? Because, according to God's prophetic timetable, the time to favour her, *the set time*, has come! (Psalm 102:13, 14).

And what is the evidence of God's mercy and favour? That after almost 1,900 years of dispersion to the four corners of the earth, the Ancient Covenant people are being regathered to the Land, and upon returning, are *'taking pleasure in her stones and showing favour to her dust.'*

In the language of the prophets, the wilderness is becoming a fruitful field, the desert is blossoming as the rose, the ancient ruins are being rebuilt, and the ruined cities are being restored.

That which is good in the sight of the Lord should also be good in the sight of His people, if indeed, we are living close to His heart.

The testimony of the Prophetic Church reads thusly: *'It seemed good to the Holy Spirit and to us . . .'* (Acts 15:28). If it is the Lord's time to favour Zion, can we, His servants, do any less?

There is a wonderful promise of prosperity to those who share God's love for Jerusalem:

> *'Pray for the peace of Jerusalem: "May they prosper who love you. Peace be within your walls, prosperity within your palaces." For the sake of my brethren and companions, I will now say, "Peace be within you." Because of the house of the LORD our God, I will seek your good.'*
>
> (Psalm 122:6–9)

The Hebrew word *'shaal'*, translated 'pray', means to *ask, inquire, request, pray, desire,* and *wish for.* It depicts those who, out of a heart of love for Jerusalem, inquire earnestly about its welfare, pray for its peace, and ask with true concern about its condition.

The 'peace' of which the Psalmist speaks is more than a mere cessation of hostilities. The Hebrew word *'shalom'* denotes wholeness in every part of life: spiritual well-being, mental and emotional stability, physical health, economic and material prosperity, and social harmony.

Of course, such peace will only be fully enjoyed when Messiah rules in Jerusalem upon the Throne of David.

But for those who desire God's best for Jerusalem and pray unceasingly for the realization of her prophetic destiny, this promise holds true: *'They shall prosper who love you; that is, they shall be happy, secure and successful!'*

Rejoice with Jerusalem!

Through the prophet Isaiah, the Lord says: *'Behold, I will do a new thing, now it shall spring forth; shall you not know it?'* (Isaiah 43:19).

The question is not of God, as to whether or not He will act; the question is of us, as to whether or not we will recognize and accept what He is doing! *'I will do a new thing, but will you know it and be part of it?'*

This is nowhere more pertinent than in respect to the restoration of Jerusalem. The prophecy of Isaiah further exhorts us to:

> *'Be glad and rejoice forever in what I create; for behold, I create Jerusalem as a rejoicing, and her people a joy. I will*

15

> *rejoice in Jerusalem, and joy in My people ... Rejoice with*
> *Jerusalem, and be glad with her, all you who love her;*
> *rejoice for joy with her, all you who mourn for her; That*
> *you may feed and be satisfied with the consolation of her*
> *bosom, that you may drink deeply and be delighted with the*
> *abundance of her glory. For thus says the LORD: Behold, I*
> *will extend peace to her like a river, and the glory of the*
> *Gentiles like a flowing stream. Then you shall feed; on her*
> *sides shall you be carried, and be dandled on her knees. As*
> *one whom his mother comforts, so I will comfort you; and*
> *you shall be comforted in Jerusalem.'*
>
> (Isaiah 65:18, 19a; 66:10–13)

The ultimate fulfilment of this Scripture is undoubtedly contained in the age to come, under Messiah's personal, righteous and universal rule.

However, as previously stated, we are living in the times of the restoration of all things (Acts 3:21). The process of restoration will continue until the end of the age and will be consummated in our Lord's Appearing and His eternal reign in the world to come.

There is no doubt, however, but that the process is presently underway. Evidence of Divine Restoration abounds in both the Church and Israel.

In the last one hundred years we have seen Jerusalem transformed from a flea-bitten, ant-ridden, country town in the Syrian province of the Ottoman Empire, into the thriving capital of a sovereign Jewish state – a capital which, in many respects, has become the epicentre of world events.

And once again, God invites a positive response on the part of His people to the work of His hands:

'Recognize what I am doing in Jerusalem. Be glad and rejoice in it. For as you comfort Jerusalem, so I will comfort you, and indeed, your comfort shall be in Jerusalem. She will suckle you; she will nurse you; she will carry you at her side and fondle you on her lap; she will be a source of unspeakable joy and a crown of glory to the whole company of the redeemed!'

When the love of God for Jerusalem is poured out in our

hearts by the Holy Spirit, we will find ourselves, perhaps unconsciously, fulfilling the exhortation of the prophet:

> '*"Comfort, yes, comfort My people!" says your God.*
> *"Speak comfort to Jerusalem, and cry out to her, that her*
> *warfare is ended, that her iniquity is pardoned; for she has*
> *received from the LORD's hand double for all her sins."*'
>
> (Isaiah 40:1, 2)

The phrase 'speak comfort' literally means, *'speak tenderly to
the heart of'*. It denotes one's innermost being – the seat of the
emotions, reason and will.

God is actually saying, *'Speak to the heart of Jerusalem, to the
very depths of her soul, to the hidden springs of her innermost
being.'*

The projected concept is one of *compassionate understanding*, issuing in *tender communication* and *sensitive touch*. The
word 'comfort' implies not just *sympathy for*, but *empathy with*.

Then, we will have truly entered into the burden of our Lord
who cried, *'Jerusalem, Jerusalem ... how often have I longed to
gather your children to Me as a hen gathers her chickens under
her wings ...'* (Matthew 23:37, Rieu).

The Anointing of Jerusalem

There is an anointing of the Holy Spirit upon the city of
Jerusalem to gather the nations and worship the Lord.

This anointing was foreshadowed under the Mosaic Covenant
with the incumbent responsibility of Jewish males to appear
before the Lord three times a year *'in the place of His choosing,'*
that is, Jerusalem, at the feasts of *Pesach*, *Shavuot*, and *Sukkot*
(Deuteronomy 16:16).

In light of this, it is interesting to note that the Holy Spirit was
poured out on Jewish pilgrims who had come up to Jerusalem to
keep the Feast of *Shavuot*, thus resulting in the birth of the
Church! (Acts 2).

The anointing of Jerusalem will have its ultimate expression
in the age to come, when representatives of all nations

> *'... go up from year to year to worship the King, the LORD of hosts, and to keep the Feast of Tabernacles. And it shall be that whichever of the families of the earth do not come up to Jerusalem to worship the King, the LORD of hosts, on them there will be no rain.'* (Zechariah 14:16, 17)

Even now, the anointing of Jerusalem is drawing believers from among the nations to worship the Lord in His holy mountain. Whether they realize it or not, these believers are engaged in a *sermo propheticus realis*, a prophetic preaching by fact.

And even now, blessings and judgments are being meted out to the nations on account of their attitude toward Jerusalem and Israel.

The Lord has blessed our local fellowship in Melbourne by sending us, on various occasions throughout the last fifteen years, servants and handmaidens who have brought the anointing of Jerusalem with them.

As they would lead us in songs of love and intercession for the city of Jerusalem and the Land of Israel, the Presence and Glory of God would fall upon the congregation.

Some of our most powerful corporate anointings have been experienced during times of 'prayer for the peace of Jerusalem'.

As a pastor, I can vouch for the fact that a church which blesses Jerusalem will itself be blessed!

References

1.   *God's Timetable for the End of Time*, by Oral Roberts. Heliotrope Publications, Tulsa, Oklahoma, p. 32.

Chapter 2

The Power of Prophetic Desire

'Hope deferred makes the heart sick, but when the desire comes, it is a tree of life.' (Proverbs 13:12)

'Brethren, my heart's desire and prayer to God for Israel is that they may be saved.' (Romans 10:1)

The year was 1894. The place, Paris, France. A young newspaper correspondent stood watching the trial of Alfred Dreyfus, a Jewish Captain serving with the French General Staff, who had been falsely accused of spying for Germany.

As the young correspondent witnessed the trial of Dreyfus and his subsequent sentencing to exile on France's notorious Devil's Island, and heard the French mob scream 'Death to the Jews', a mixture of fear and horror gripped his heart.

'If this could happen in Paris, where Jews have been free for over one hundred years,' thought the young observer, 'it could happen anywhere.' He recognized the imperative need for Jews to settle, as a nation among nations, in a state of their own. And so the dream of a regathered people and a recreated nation began to take shape.

The name of the lawyer-come-correspondent was Theodor Herzl, an Austro-Hungarian Jew from Budapest. Herzl was not a religious man, but there is no doubt that his dream of a sovereign Jewish State in *Eretz* Israel was inspired of God.

After the first World Zionist Congress in Basel, Switzerland, in 1897, Herzl wrote in his diary,

> *'At Basel I founded the Jewish State. If I were to say this today, I would be greeted with laughter. In five years perhaps and certainly in fifty, everyone will see it.'*

Exactly fifty years later, on November 29th, 1947, Herzl's dream was voted into reality by the United Nations.

Herzl was a man of mission and destiny. When he was dying, he called for one of his close friends, William Hechler, Chaplain of the British Embassy in Vienna.

The Zionist leader told Hechler that when he was twelve years old, he had a dream in which he saw a man who appeared very old but full of majesty. The man said to him, 'I have raised you up that you might be the means of bringing My people together again from the ends of the earth.'

Herzl died in 1904 as a result of heart disease, overwork and stress. For many Zionists, Herzl's untimely death signalled the end of their aspirations and dreams. William Hechler, however, took a different view. He declared, 'God has taken away Herzl to show us that the Jews will reach their salvation through God alone, even without so great a man as Herzl.'

It should be pointed out, however, that the dream of a Jewish homeland in *Eretz* Israel was not unique to Theodor Herzl or to his generation. Throughout the centuries Jews hoped and prayed for the regathering of the exiles and the restoration of Zion. Year after year in the Passover ceremony they would exclaim, 'Next year in Jerusalem!'

But the wheels of restoration did not begin to really turn until the latter part of the 19th century.

After 1,800 years of dispersion among the nations of the world, Israel was indeed, a Divine Idea whose time had arrived. And God began to raise up men and women, in accordance with His purpose, as instruments of restoration.

Christian Zionists

The Bible holds the key to understanding God's purposes for Israel. The Holy Scriptures are 'God-breathed', that is, they are imbued with His Spirit and Life (2 Timothy 3:16; John 6:63). As one meditates in the Word, one partakes of the Divine Nature and begins to act in accordance with the Divine will and purpose (2 Peter 1:4).

Indeed, a revelation of God's timeless love for the Jewish people and His end-time purpose for the nation of Israel transforms one's attitude and behaviour!

This principle was clearly demonstrated in England in the 16th Century. The Jews had been expelled from England some 300 years before, fleeing mostly to France and Flanders, their property and belongings being confiscated by the British.

Throughout this time, the Christian Church in England was as guilty as any group of anti-semitic attitudes and actions.

However, the translation of the Bible into English (the language of the people) in the 16th and 17th centuries and a growing hunger for spiritual reality in the English Church transformed the religious climate of the nation, and hence, the attitude of many Christians toward the Jewish people. Zeal for doctrinal purity and devotion to the total reformation of the Church earned these Christians the name *Puritans*.

Scholars and laymen alike were awakened to the authority and relevancy of Scripture, and with that awakening came a fresh understanding of God's purposes for the People and Land of Israel. At long last, the light of God's Word began to shine in the darkness of religious bigotry.

So began the 'Restoration Movement' – a spontaneous and significant movement of the Holy Spirit in the Christian Church which, interestingly enough, became one of the catalysts and supporting pillars of the Zionist movement.

However, the 17th and 18th centuries saw the emergence of the 'Age of Reason', in which Puritanism was supplanted in many areas of society by Rationalism and its religious offspring Deism. Rationalists disputed the Divine inspiration of Scripture, the personal revelation of God, the literalness of Bible prophecy and the miracles of Jesus, and of course, the Deity of Messiah.

The battle for the soul of the British people, and in a peculiar sense, the prophetic destiny of the nation of Israel, continued as God moved by His Spirit through the apostolic preaching of

John Wesley and George Whitefield. A new generation of believers rose up who took God's Word seriously and realized, among other things, that God was not finished with the Jewish people.

Interest in the restoration of the Jews, and indeed, in the whole vista of eschatology intensified following the outbreak of the French Revolution in 1789. Englishmen began to hear and to read that the tumultuous events across the Channel heralded the end of the generations and the impending advent of the Kingdom of Messiah.

A prophetic book of that day, *Signs of the Times* by James Bicheno, stated that the upheaval in Europe signalled the beginning of the latter days, a period of time that would see the return of the Jews to their ancient homeland in unbelief and their subsequent turning to Jesus as their Messiah.

Christian interest in the restoration of the Jews further increased in 1798, following Napoleon's invasion of Egypt and 'Palestine'. Napoleon was defeated by Sir Sidney Smith and the British Fleet at the Battle of Acre in 1799, at which point the Eastern Mediterranean began to play an important role in British foreign policy. Prophetic-minded evangelical Christians who had understanding of the times began to predict that Britain would henceforth be used by God in assisting the restoration of the Jews.

The evangelical revival of the 18th and 19th centuries lit a fire of missionary zeal among God's people and gave birth to a number of Gospel societies, among the most popular of which was the **London Society for Promoting Christianity Among the Jews**.

In 1824, the Jews' Society proposed that a British Consulate be established in Jerusalem to protect the rights of Protestant Christians and Jews, the latter of which were beaten, jailed and fined with impunity under Turkish Ottoman law. This proposal was realized some fifteen years later with the appointment of Consul William Tanner Young. The consulate was established on the property of the Jews' Society, just inside Jaffa Gate opposite the Citadel, where *Christ Church* was later to be built.

Meanwhile, the Jews' Society was actively involved in evangelizing the Jewish population of Jerusalem. **John Nicolayson**, a

Danish-born, LJS-trained missionary, wrote in 1839 of the baptism of the family of one Simon Rosenthal:

> 'I had then the happiness of baptizing this whole family, as the first Israelitish family that, in all probability, has been baptized in this city since the early Christian times – thus grafted in again into their own olive tree, thus laying once more the first living stones of a Hebrew-Christian Church at Jerusalem, on the same apostolic foundation first laid here on the great first day of Pentecost.'[1]

Take special note of the words, 'the first living stones of a Hebrew-Christian Church at Jerusalem on the same apostolic foundation first laid here on the great first day of Pentecost'. This epitomizes the prophetic vision of John Nicolayson and his LJS colleagues, a vision that was finally realized some one hundred and fifty years later, through the ministry of Kehilah HaMashiach, the Messianic congregation that meets at Christ Church!

The Jew's Society, under the inspiration and direction of the Seventh Earl of Shaftesbury, **Anthony Ashley Cooper**, also established an Anglican Bishopric in Jerusalem as part of an overall strategy to regather the Jewish people and restore the Jewish homeland, in the belief that such action would, in accordance with the Prophetic Word, prepare the way for Messiah's return.

Another example of the prophetic insight of these early pioneers is contained in the minutes of the annual general meeting of the Jews' Society, held on May 6th, 1841, in which Lord Shaftesbury elucidated the goals of the Jewish mission:

> '... in Palestine you will give them the means of obtaining an honest livelihood, and perhaps the monopoly of practical science through the length and breadth of their own land. But this result is more than probably – that there you will be raising up a body of Missionaries, whose successes will far eclipse the successes of the Gentiles, and who will show to us practically, what we have long known by precept, but have forgotten in practice, that the Gospel of

Christ, to be finally successful, must be preached among all nations in His name, "beginning at Jerusalem." [2]

The first Bishop of Jerusalem was a former Jewish rabbi, **Michael Solomon Alexander**. His entry into the city on January 21st, 1842, signalled the beginning of restoration: Of the Jews to the Land, of the Jewish people to the Messiah, and of the Church to its Jewish origins.

The 'Jewish Church' and its related ministries contributed practically and materially as well as spiritually to the Jewish and Arab communities of Jerusalem.

On December 12th, 1844, the Jews' Society opened a 'Hospital for Poor Sick Jews' – the first hospital in the modern history of Jerusalem. But despite stiff rabbinical opposition (which included the issuing of a *cherem* – an anathema against any Jewish person who entered the hospital), the medical work continued and eventually transformed the public health system of Jerusalem.

The first house of industry in Jerusalem was opened by Bishop Alexander in 1843, where Jewish men learned a trade and received religious instruction. The olive wood industry began in this institution. A Hebrew College for the training of Hebrew Christian missionaries was also opened in 1843, teaching such subjects as divinity, English, German, Hebrew, arithmetic, music and language translation.

Significant contributions were also made in such areas as children's education, agriculture, architecture and engineering, so much so, that Jewish philanthropists like Sir Moses Montefiore and Baron Edmond de Rothschild were provoked to jealousy and galvanized to action!

Benjamin Disraeli (Lord Beaconsfield) was a Jewish man who embraced the Christian faith. He is considered to be one of the greatest statesmen the Jewish people have ever produced, serving on two occasions as Prime Minister of Great Britain which, at that time, boasted the most powerful and extensive empire in the world.

Disraeli's pride in and insistence upon his Jewish ancestry raised the ire of his opponents in Parliament, and even bred

mistrust amongst his own followers. He played a significant part
in the parliamentary struggle for Jewish emancipation, as evi-
denced by his contribution to the debate on Jewish Disabilities:

> 'The Jews are persons who acknowledge the same God as
> the Christian people of this realm. They acknowledge the
> same Divine revelations as yourselves ... they are,
> humanly speaking, the authors of your religion. They are
> unquestionably those to whom you are indebted for no
> inconsiderable portion of your known religion and for the
> whole of your Divine knowledge ...
>
> 'Where is your Christianity, if you do not believe in their
> Judaism? On every sacred day, you read to the people the
> exploits of Jewish heroes, the proofs of Jewish devotion,
> the brilliant annals of past Jewish magnificence. The
> Christian Church has covered every kingdom with sacred
> buildings, and over every altar ... we find the tables of the
> Jewish Law. Every Sunday – every Lord's Day – if you
> wish to express feelings of praise and thanksgiving to the
> Most High, or if you wish to find expressions of solace in
> grief, you find both in the words of Jewish poets ... Every
> man in the early ages of the Church, by whose power, or
> zeal, or genius, the Christian faith was propagated, was a
> Jew ...
>
> 'I, whatever may be the consequences – must speak what
> I feel. I cannot sit in this house with any misconception of
> my opinion on the subject. Whatever may be the con-
> sequences on the seat I hold ... I cannot, for one, give a
> vote which is not in deference to what I believe to be the
> true principles of religion. Yes, it is as a Christian that I will
> not take upon me the awful responsibility of excluding
> from the Legislature those who are of the religion in the
> bosom of which my Lord and Saviour was born.'[3]

Disraeli continued to promote, through precept and personal
example, the historical link between Judaism and Christianity.
Moreover, he was a romantic Zionist at heart. In his novel
Tancred – an exposition of the debt of gratitude which European civilization, and the English Church in particular, owed to

the Jews as the founder of their religious faith – he talks of 'those days of political justice when Jerusalem belonged to the Jews.' In private conversation he envisaged 'the recolonizing of Palestine by the Jews.'

Disraeli was reportedly 'thunderstruck' at his first sight of Jerusalem, and once said of Palestine, 'To touch her is to touch eternity.'

Sir Laurence Oliphant was one of the most colourful and versatile supporters of the Zionist movement. He served as a soldier, diplomat, author, journalist, and Member of the British Parliament, as well as being a scholar of Russian language and culture.

In about 1878, Oliphant became aware of the plight of European Jewry and set out with characteristic zeal to secure for them 'the land of Gilead' east of the Jordan River.

Due to a change of Government and foreign policy in Britain, Oliphant was unable to fulfil his dream, and the dream of European Jews and British Restorationists – the establishment of a Jewish State in Palestine.

However, not to be thwarted, Oliphant joined forces with a group called *Hovevei Zion* (Lovers of Zion), started by Jewish intellectuals in Russia who recognized that assimilation would not save them from the pogroms that were sweeping across Europe, destroying Jewish lives and property with reckless abandon.

As Russian Jews in small numbers began making their way to Palestine, Oliphant and his wife left the comforts of England and settled in Haifa to be on hand to assist the new arrivals. He died there in 1888, having lived to see new agricultural settlements established by these refugees from persecution.

Sir Laurence Oliphant was a man who received a revelation of God's end-time purpose for Israel and responded by devoting the rest of his life to the fulfilment of the vision. As such, he is an outstanding example for believers of this generation, to whom much has been given and of whom much is required!

Another outstanding man who served the purposes of God in his generation was **William Hechler**, chaplain of the British Embassy in Vienna.

An Anglican clergyman and son of a Hebrew scholar, Hechler became convinced from his study of Bible prophecy that 1897 was the crucial year for the restoration of the Jewish State. When he read Theodor Herzl's book, *Der Judenstaat* (The Jewish State), three weeks after its publication in 1896, he went directly to the author and put himself at his disposal to facilitate the vision.

Hechler was instrumental in arranging an audience for Herzl with Frederic, Grand Duke of Baden, and through Frederic, meetings with Kaiser Wilhelm of Germany. He also arranged for his bishop to bless Herzl and the Zionist movement. Hechler's tireless efforts and prayers opened several significant doors for Herzl, and ultimately for Zionism.

When the World Zionist Congress met in 1903 to consider Uganda as an alternative homeland for the Jews, Hechler, an unofficial participant, was one of those who argued that accepting the British proposal would save some lives but might forever preclude resettlement in their own true homeland.

After World War One Hechler implored the Jews to leave Europe, warning them of the impending tragedy, prophesying that they would soon be slaughtered by the millions!

Hechler devoted thirty years of his life to the Zionist movement. Although he did not live to see its eventual manifestation, Hechler played a strategic role in the rebirth of the State of Israel.

His faith and vision are enshrined in the words he wrote to the Grand Duke of Baden on the occasion of the Duke's 70th birthday:

> 'According to the Bible the Jews must return to Palestine, and I therefore help this movement as a Christian and in complete faith for the truth of the Bible, for this is the cause of God.'[4]

World War One broke out in 1914 and lasted approximately four years. The most significant event of the entire war took place on December 11th, 1917, when **General Edmund Allenby** captured Jerusalem from the Turks, thus ending the 400 year-long rule of the Ottoman Empire.

Allenby took the city without firing a shot. Indeed, it was as if Almighty God, who controls the times and seasons, had determined to end the Turkish occupation of the Land, and thus, judicially handed the stewardship of His City to Great Britain, in the person of Edmund Allenby.

It is interesting to note the manner and spirit in which Allenby, a God-fearing Christian, received the sacred trust of the City of God. He rode up to the Jaffa Gate, dismounted from his horse, and entered Jerusalem on foot, declaring that 'no one but the Messiah should enter this city mounted!'

Allenby entered Jerusalem on the first day of *Hanukkah*, the Festival that commemorates the deliverance of the Jewish people from the oppression of Antiochus Epiphanes in the Second Century BC. To the Jews of Jerusalem, Allenby's triumphant ingress on this day of all days was a sign of Redemption.

The emancipation of Jerusalem was celebrated on the steps near David's Citadel in the presence of troops from the Australian Light Horse who had played such an important role in the Battle of Beersheva and the liberation of the Holy Land.

This in itself was a prophetic sign that the redemptive purpose of God was coming full circle. At the beginning of the 'Church Age' Jesus dispatched His emissaries from Jerusalem to Judea, Samaria, and the uttermost parts of the earth (Acts 1:8).

Almost 2,000 years later, in the last of the last days, representatives from the 'uttermost parts' (Australia and New Zealand) were returning to bless Jerusalem, and albeit unconsciously, to consummate the purposes of God!

What began at Jerusalem on the Day of Pentecost must, of necessity, finish at Jerusalem.

At the beginning of this age Jerusalem blessed the nations by sending forth her apostles and prophets with the Gospel of Messiah; so, at the end of this age, the nations will return to bless Jerusalem – *naturally*, as in the case of General Allenby and his troops, and *spiritually*, with the Power and Presence of God!

Another interesting sidelight to this whole event was the role that the Royal Air Force played in the fulfilment of prophecy! Some 2,500 years earlier the prophet Isaiah had written:

> *'Like birds flying about, so will the* LORD *of hosts defend Jerusalem. Defending, He will also deliver it; passing over, He will preserve it.'* (Isaiah 31:5)

Prior to Allenby's arrival, aircraft of the Royal Air Force 14 Squadron flew over Jerusalem dropping leaflets, written in Arabic, which commanded the people to surrender. Allenby's name resembled that of the Islamic deity, and many Moslem inhabitants perceived that *Allah* was commanding submission!

As if patterned on the words of Isaiah, 14 Squadron's motto was: 'I spread my wings to keep it.'

One month earlier, on November 2nd, 1917, a letter had been delivered in London to Lord Rothschild from British Foreign Secretary **Arthur James Balfour**, which read in part:

> 'I have much pleasure in conveying to you, on behalf of His Majesty's Government, the following declaration of sympathy with Jewish Zionist aspirations ... His Majesty's Government view with favour the establishment in Palestine of a national home for the Jewish people and will use their best endeavours to facilitate the achievement of this object, it being clearly understood that nothing shall be done which may prejudice the civil and religious rights of existing and non-Jewish communities in Palestine, or the rights and political status enjoyed by Jews in any other country.'

Balfour was born in Scotland in 1848 and raised in an evangelical family. He read and studied the Bible from early childhood and consequently possessed a profound interest in the Jews and a strong belief in the regathering of the exiles and the rebirth of the Jewish State.

His mother eagerly awaited the Second Coming of the Lord and taught her son that 'the Jew must first return to Palestine and then will come the final consummation.'

29

Balfour once said:

> 'The ideal that most moves me is that Christendom ... is not unmindful of the service which the Jews have rendered and that we desire ... to give them the opportunity of developing in peace and quietness ... those great gifts they have been compelled to bring to fruition ... in countries which know not their language and belong not to their race.'[5]

Moreover, he said that he valued this involvement above all others in a fifty year career that included service as Prime Minister.

In 1925 Lord Balfour attended the opening ceremony of the Hebrew University on Mount Scopus in Jerusalem. He died five years later and never saw the ultimate fulfilment of his prophetic declaration. However, there is no doubt but that the little piece of paper known in history as *'the Balfour Declaration'* opened the way for the Jewish State to come into being just three decades later!

His 'declaration of sympathy with Jewish Zionist aspirations' was the modern day equivalent of the Proclamation of Cyrus which authorized the Jews to return to the Land of their fathers and rebuild the Lord's House in Jerusalem (Ezra 1:1–4).

Finally, one could not forget the invaluable contribution of British Army Captain (and later, Major-General) **Orde Charles Wingate**. Born in India and related to Lawrence of Arabia, Wingate was consumed by twin passions: military science and the Bible. He was a deeply religious man and a committed Christian, who gained a reputation for always carrying a Bible under his arm.

Wingate was posted to Palestine in 1936 and developed a life-long love for and empathy with Zionism. Describing his first encounters with the Jewish Community, he wrote: 'I felt I belonged to such a people.'

Soon after his arrival in Palestine, Wingate explained to a Jewish military commander that his sympathies were with Zionism, declaring with characteristic emphasis, 'There is only one important book on the subject, the Bible, and I have read it thoroughly!'

At Wingate's recommendation, special night squads of Jewish and British soldiers were formed to operate against Arab terrorists. Together with *Haganah* commander Yitzhak Sadeh, Wingate trained these young Jewish volunteers in the rudiments of guerilla warfare: secrecy, surprise, mobile ambushes and hand-to-hand fighting, combined with a determination to always take the initiative.

Writing to his cousin, Sir Reginald Wingate, he said: 'I have seen Jewish youth in the Kibbutzim, and I assure you that the Jews will produce soldiers better than ours.'

Known in the *Haganah* as 'The Friend', Wingate instilled in his charges an undying sense of comradeship and openly voiced his faith in the future of the Jewish nation:

> 'This is the cause of your survival. I count it as my privilege to help you fight your battle. To that purpose I want to devote my life. I believe that the very existence of mankind is justified when it is based on the moral foundation of the Bible. Whoever dares lift a hand against you and your enterprise here should be fought against. Whether it is jealousy, ignorance or perverted doctrine such as have made your neighbours rise against you, or "politics" which make some of my countrymen support them, I shall fight with you against any of these influences. But remember that it is your battle. My part, which I say I feel to be a privilege, is only to help you.'[6]

Wingate's friendship with and support for the Jews incurred the wrath of the British Mandatory Government, which consistently sought to protect its own vested interests and appease the demands of the Arab Higher Committee at the expense of Jewish lives and property.

The Army transferred Wingate from the Land, stamping his passport 'Not allowed to enter Palestine.' Standing before his men shortly before his departure, Wingate said in halting Hebrew: 'I am sent away from you and the country I love ...

they want to hurt me and you. I promise you that I will come back, and if I cannot do it the regular way, I shall return as a refugee.'

Wingate was eventually killed in an aircrash in Burma in 1944, whilst training and leading troops operating behind enemy lines. But the 'Maccabee spirit' which he had imparted to his charges from the Kibbutzim lived on.

Thus, it was 'mission accomplished' for Orde Wingate. In just a few short years he had done precisely what God had brought him to the Land to do. As stated in his own words at the opening of a Jewish Sergeants course in 1938: 'Remember, we are here to found a Jewish Army!'

Of course, there were many other righteous Gentiles, lovers of Zion and of the God of Israel, who believed the promises, perceived the fulfilment of prophecy in their generation, and became a part of what God was doing in Zion.

Devout Christians such as the **ten Boom family** of Holland, risked their lives to shelter Jewish refugees from the ferocious Nazi beast. Some remained undetected, others managed to escape, and others, including some Jewish children, were successfully smuggled into Palestine. But if caught sheltering or aiding Jews, both the refugees and their Christian protectors were arrested and sent to Concentration Camps.

Eternity alone will reveal the faithful watchmen who interceded day and night for Zion, and gave of their time, money and resources in the struggle for the rebirth of Israel.

> '"They shall be Mine," says the Lord of hosts, "on the day that I make them My jewels. And I will spare them as a man spares his own son who serves him."'   (Malachi 3:17)

Servants of God's Purpose

Throughout the latter part of Turkish-Ottoman rule and the three decades of British Mandatory Government (1917–1948), various people made significant contributions to the Zionist cause. Some are now recognized as household names. Others are less well-known and some are virtually unknown, yet their contributions were nonetheless important.

Sir Moses Montefiore, a Jewish banker and philanthropist, was Sheriff of London when Queen Victoria acceded to the Throne in 1837. He visited the Holy Land seven times, making his last trip at the age of ninety!

Montefiore visited Jerusalem which, up until that time was contained within the imposing walls erected by Suleiman the Magnificent between 1537 and 1541. The Old City was divided into four nearly equal parts – Jewish, Armenian, Muslim and Christian.

Montefiore saw the potential for further development beyond the walls, and secured for the Jews a plot of ground on the western slopes of the city. He also gave liberally toward improving the supply of water to the city.

Today, a famous windmill stands in the suburb of *Yemin-Moshe*, overlooking the walls of the Old City, as a memorial to the Founder of Modern Jerusalem.

In 1870, a small group of courageous Romanian Jews founded a village on the coastal plain, north of Jaffa, called **Petach Tikvah** (Gateway of Hope). Petach Tikvah was soon joined by a cluster of other similar Jewish settlements, which became the first outposts of the Return.

The pioneers of these settlements came to be known as members of 'the First *Aliyah*' (the Hebrew word for ascending, or going up to Zion, and the modern word for a wave of immigration).

The Second *Aliyah*, which settled in the Land between 1904 and 1914, eventually brought some 50,000 European Jews to Palestine. The Second *Aliyah* pioneered two unique forms of rural group living – the *kibbutz*, of which the prototype was **Deganiah**, founded in 1909 on the southern shore of the Sea of Galilee, and the *Moshav*.

Another important aspect of the Second *Aliyah* was the formation of *Hashomer* (the Hebrew word for 'watchmen'), forerunner of the Israel Defence Force, in 1907.

Yitzhak Ben Zvi (who later became Israel's second President) was one of the Watchmen, who, together with his fellow pioneers, solemnly swore loyalty to the Jewish national cause and to each other, thereby founding an organization to protect isolated Jewish settlements from Arab marauders.

Eliezer Ben-Yehuda, an immigrant from Lithuania, was primarily responsible for the restoration of Hebrew as the language of the people.

He meticulously compiled a dictionary, seeking to include all the words needed for contemporary living, and began to speak only Hebrew himself, making his wife and children follow suit.

Years before he had written: 'Hebrew did not die of exhaustion; it died with the nation. When the nation revives, it will live again.'

In 1909, a frustrated group of pioneers, stirred to action by **Meir Dizengoff**, bought 32 acres of sand dunes a little distance from the old Arab port of Jaffa. The idea was to establish a new, wholly Jewish suburb, and digging began at what is now the intersection of Rothschild Boulevard and Herzl Street.

Today, Tel Aviv is the largest completely Jewish city in the world, and Jaffa is one of its suburbs!

Joseph Trumpeldor and **Vladimir (Ze'ev) Jabotinsky**, both Russian Jews, formed the 'Jewish Legion' which served with the British forces in Palestine in the latter stages of World War One.

Both believed that if the Jews wanted to reclaim Palestine as their national homeland, then, as in the past, they would have to fight for it.

Trumpeldor died in 1921, leading the defence of Tel Hai, a northern settlement overrun by Arabs. Jabotinsky went on to found the militant Zionist Revisionist Movement.

Golda Meir, the most famous woman in modern Jewish history, served with distinction in the *Histadrut* (Jewish Federation of Labour), and later as Israel's first envoy to Moscow, then as Labour Minister, then as Foreign Minister, and finally as Prime Minister.

During the dark and desperate days that preceded the establishment of the State, Golda Meir travelled to the USA to inform American Jewry of the needs of the *Yishuv* (the Jewish community of Palestine). She addressed Jewish groups and organizations across the country, appealing for funds to finance the purchase of arms in Europe by the *Haganah* (the Jewish Defence Force).

The response from both Jews and Christians was overwhelming. Within six weeks over fifty million dollars had been raised, prompting David Ben-Gurion to say, 'Some day when history will be written, it will be said that there was a Jewish woman who got the money which made the State possible.'

The mantle of Zionist leadership eventually fell upon the broad shoulders of **Dr Chaim Weizmann**. Weizmann was born in the Russian city of Pinsk, but spent much of his life living and working in England. A noted scientist and a distinguished statesman, Weizmann played an important role in the securing of the Balfour Declaration.

Dr Weizmann served as President of the World Zionist Organization from 1920 to 1931, and again from 1935 to 1946. His meeting with US President Harry Truman in April, 1948, persuaded the American leader to recognize the emerging State of Israel.

In February, 1949, Weizmann was installed as Israel's first President, a post he held until his death in 1952.

Probably the best known Jewish leader of modern times is **David Ben-Gurion**. Born in Poland in 1886, he immigrated to Palestine in 1906 and helped to lay the foundation of the *Histadrut* and the Labour Party, and eventually became its virtually unchallenged leader and boss.

Ben-Gurion served as Chairman of the Jewish Agency, and later as the first Prime Minister of the State of Israel. He gave practical and moral leadership to the *Yishuv* during the tragic years of Nazi domination in Europe and the crucial days leading up to the termination of the British Mandate in Palestine.

Ben-Gurion's character was anchored in the Bible. It was his principal source of inspiration. He used it as his guide in the pursuit of Zionist goals and the setting of moral standards.

> '"Nothing can surpass the Bible at lighting up the manifold problems of our life," he said. "There can be no worthwhile political or military education about Israel without profound knowledge of the Bible."'[7]

From early childhood, Ben-Gurion regularly immersed himself in the Bible, and his love for the Book never dimmed

35

through the years. His large, black Bible always accompanied him wherever he went, and was often opened at his favourite book, the Prophecy of Isaiah. He frequently read the words of the prophets which spoke of the regathering of the exiles and the rebuilding of Zion.

From the eternal promises of an unchanging God, Ben-Gurion gained strength and courage to face the seemingly insurmountable obstacles that stood between the little Jewish remnant and Statehood.

He once declared:

> 'I know that God promised all of Palestine to the children of Israel. I do not know what borders He set. I believe that they are wider than the ones proposed. If God will keep His promise in His own time, our business as poor humans who live in a difficult age is to save as much as we can of the remnants of Israel . . .'[8]

Ben-Gurion was by no means perfect. His marriage problems, alleged moral failures and experimentation with Eastern religions attest to that.

However, there is no doubt but that David Ben-Gurion, like his British contemporary Winston Churchill, was a man of destiny who had 'come to the kingdom for such a time as this.'

Besides the above mentioned leaders were thousands of unsung heroes whose names we may never know, each of whom, in his or her own way, helped to forge the establishment of the State of Israel.

Courageous pioneers who drained the swamplands, tilled the soil and turned the wilderness into a garden.

Valiant young men and women who defended the Kibbutzim and helped to supply the beleaguered city of Jerusalem with food and arms during the last tremulous days of the British Mandate.

Brave souls who helped smuggle Jewish refugees into Palestine during the dark days of World War Two, thereby saving multitudes from a certain death.

And finally, the survivors of the Holocaust, who miraculously escaped the satanic fury of Hitler's 'Final Solution' and made their way to *Eretz* Israel in search of an identity and a destiny, in spite of the apathy of the United Nations, the militant opposition of the Arabs, and the blatant partiality of the British Mandatory Government.

These 'servants of God's purpose' had one thing in common – a dream that was as old as the Bible itself – a prophetic desire for the restoration of Zion!

References

1. 'Report of the London Society for Promoting Christianity Amongst the Jews', 1839, p. 75, as quoted in *For the Love of Zion* by Kelvin Crombie, Hodder & Stoughton, p. 25.
2. 'Jewish Intelligence', 1841, p. 161, as quoted in *For the Love of Zion* by Kelvin Crombie, Hodder & Stoughton, p. 34.
3. *Disraeli* by Sarah Bradford (quoting Hansard), Weidenfeld and Nicolson, London.
4. 'A Memory of the Early Zionists' by Henriette Hannah Bodenheimer, from *Christian Zionism and its Biblical Basis*, International Christian Embassy Jerusalem.
5. *A History of Israel* by Rinna Samuel, Weidenfeld and Nicolson, London, p. 37.
6. *Gideon Goes to War* by Leonard Mosley, Arthur Barker Ltd, London.
7. *Ben-Gurion Prophet of Fire* by Dan Kurzman, Simon and Schuster, p. 26.
8. *Whose Promised Land?* by Murray Dixon, Heinemann Education, p. 56.

Chapter 3

The Presence of the Miraculous

> *'Men of Israel, hear these words: Jesus of Nazareth, a man attested by God to you by miracles, wonders and signs which God did through Him in your midst...'*
>
> (Acts 2:22)

The events surrounding the rebirth of Israel and her subsequent growth and development have been remarkable, to say the least. The only reasonable explanation for her continued survival in the face of such radical opposition is the Providence of God.

It is only as we contemplate natural events in the light of God's supernatural dealings that we can understand the secret of Israel's success.

A 'miracle' occurs when the supernatural realm of God's power intercedes in the natural realm of man's need, and indeed, the modern history of Israel abounds with examples of God's miraculous provision and protection.

It is important to note, however, that the Presence of the Miraculous does not proscribe hard work and sacrifice. On the contrary, the Bible declares that *'God is a rewarder of those who diligently seek Him'* (Hebrews 11:6).

Throughout history God has consistently used the weak, insignificant and foolish things of the world to confound the mighty.

When faced with the seemingly impossible task of leading the children of Israel out of Egypt, Moses offered God all that he had – his shepherd's staff.

The little stick represented the sum total of Moses' life up until that point of time. But with the anointing of the Holy Spirit it performed signs and wonders in Egypt, parted the Red Sea, and brought the children of Israel to the border of Canaan.

Likewise, when a little boy was confronted with the needs of five thousand hungry men, he offered Jesus all that He had – five loaves and two fishes. Yet, in the hands of the Master, this insignificant portion was transformed into an enormous banquet!

On May 14th, 1948, in the midst of a raging sea of hostility, Israel became a nation. The following day at dawn, the fledgling State was attacked by five Arab armies, bent on the destruction of the Jewish people and the confiscation of their land.

For all intents and purposes, it was a hopeless mis-match. Israel, with 650,000 inhabitants including 35,000 trained troops of the *Haganah*, nine aircraft, homemade mortars and an assortment of light arms found herself battling against the combined forces of five nations, representing some forty million people, equipped with modern, sophisticated weapons.

But like David of old who dared to challenge the Philistine champion Goliath, Israel's strength and security did not lie in her natural weaponry or lack thereof, but in the Name of the Lord!

Israel's victory in the War of Independence was an amazing miracle and was the culmination of a series of miraculous events which began in 1947 in a little cave near the Dead Sea.

The Dead Sea Scrolls

It happened in the Spring of 1947. A young Bedouin was tending his goats in the barren foothills of the Judean wilderness, west of the Dead Sea. Realizing that one of his goats was missing, the young shepherd went searching for it in a steep valley near a ruin which the Arabs called *Khirbet Qumran*.

As he searched for the goat, the boy threw a stone into a hillside cave and heard what sounded to him like the breaking of pottery. Calling his assistant, the excited shepherd entered the cave and found some pottery jars 25 to 29 inches high and about 10 inches wide.

In these, they found objects that looked much like miniature mummies, but were actually leather scrolls wrapped in squares of linen cloth, and covered over with a pitch-like substance possibly derived from the Dead Sea.

With a vague idea that they had discovered *antikas* which might bring them money, the boys divided the scrolls and set off for Bethlehem where they located an antique dealer and offered him the scrolls for twenty pounds. However, he refused them.

Eventually, some of the scrolls found their way to Dr John C. Trever of the American Schools of Oriental Research who photographed them and then sent copies to Dr W.F. Albright of Johns Hopkins University (USA). This well-known authority tentatively dated them 'about 100 BC' and declared them 'an amazing discovery.'

The most important and best-preserved of all the scrolls was the Scroll of Isaiah, written in an early form of the 'square letter' which, according to Dr Albright, places it in the Second Century BC, thus making it the oldest known complete Hebrew manuscript of any Biblical book, pre-dating by at least 1,000 years the hitherto earliest known Hebrew manuscripts.

These manuscripts had been lovingly copied and hidden away by the Essene Community who lived at Qumran, just prior to the onslaught of the Roman Tenth Legion in AD 70.

The Temple had been looted and burned, Jerusalem lay in ruins, and the Roman army was marching on the last citadel of Jewish resistance at Masada. Meanwhile, the Word of God which spoke of the return of the Jewish people and the rebirth of the Jewish nation, slept peacefully in a cave, awaiting its appointed time of fulfilment.

For almost 1,900 years the desert was sanctuary to the Word of God which *'lives and abides forever'* and *'does not return void'*. During this period, known as 'the times of the Gentiles,' the Holy Land was invaded and occupied by no less than fifteen foreign powers!

Yet through it all the promise of God, like Masada itself, stood firm – a mountain of enduring hope in a wilderness of constant change and uncertainty:

> 'It shall come to pass in that day that the LORD shall set His hand again the second time to recover the remnant of His people who are left ... He will set up a banner for the nations, and will assemble the outcasts of Israel, and gather together the dispersed of Judah from the four corners of the earth.'
> (Isaiah 11:11a, 12)

And moreover,

> 'So the ransomed of the LORD shall return, and come to Zion with singing, with everlasting joy on their heads; they shall obtain joy and gladness, and sorrow and sighing shall flee away.'
> (Isaiah 51:3, 11)

And finally,

> 'How beautiful upon the mountains are the feet of him who brings good news, who proclaims peace, who brings good tidings of good things, who proclaims salvation, who says to Zion, "Your God reigns!" Your watchmen shall lift up their voices, with their voices they shall sing together; for they shall see eye to eye when the LORD brings back Zion. Break forth into joy, sing together, you waste places of Jerusalem! For the LORD has comforted His people, He has redeemed Jerusalem. The LORD has made bare His holy arm in the eyes of all the nations; and all the ends of the earth shall see the salvation of our God.'
> (Isaiah 52:7–10)

The times and seasons are in God's hands – nothing ever happens by chance. God Himself orchestrated the coincidence of the discovery of the Dead Sea Scrolls and the rebirth of the State of Israel as a sign to the world that Zion is being rebuilt fairly and squarely on the foundation of His Prophetic Word!

The miraculous events of 1947–48 once again prove that God

is Sovereign and His promises are true, and that whatever He purposes and declares will surely come to pass, despite the passage of time, the edicts of kings, and the armaments of nations!

The United Nations

The second great miracle connected with the rebirth of Israel took place on November 29th, 1947.

The British Government, whose position in Palestine had become untenable, handed the 'problem' of a Jewish homeland over to the United Nations.

UNSCOP (The United Nations Special Committee on Palestine) came to the Land, talked to everyone concerned (except the Arabs who refused to acknowledge it), met with leaders of the Arab States, and visited Germany and Austria to see the pitiful condition of over 4,500 illegal Jewish immigrants (including 2,000 children) who had arrived in Palestine in July, 1947, aboard the *'SS Exodus'*, only to be forcibly repatriated by British troops.

Finally, on August 31st, 1947, UNSCOP issued a report recommending the termination of the British Mandate, the partition of Palestine into an Arab State and a Jewish State, economic union for the whole country, and the awarding of a special status to Jerusalem as an 'international city'.

On November 29th, 1947, the UNSCOP Majority Report was voted on by the United Nations General Assembly in New York.

The British were confident the motion would be defeated and that as a result, the responsibility of the Land would be thrust back into their hands, thereby absolving them from any ongoing moral commitment to the Balfour Declaration and giving them the freedom to impose a partisan solution.

The Arabs, likewise, were confident the motion would be defeated and that one way or another, politically or militarily, they would assume control of the Land.

The Jews, after several days of intense lobbying and praying, held their breath and hoped for a miracle.

To the amazement of some, the dismay of others, and the inexpressible joy of a few, thirty-three countries voted 'Yes', thirteen voted 'No', and ten, including Great Britain abstained. Thus, the way was prepared politically for the establishment of a Jewish homeland in accordance with God's Prophetic Word!

The Bible declares that Jesus Christ is the Ruler over the kings of the earth (Revelation 1:5). God puts the desire in the hearts of kings and rulers to fulfil His purpose (Revelation 17:17). He changes men's minds and makes their thoughts conform to His will. Indeed, *'the king's heart is in the hand of the Lord, like the rivers of water; He turns it wherever He wishes'* (Proverbs 21:1).

God's sovereignty over men and nations was never more perfectly demonstrated than in the United Nations General Assembly on November 29th, 1947.

One of Israel's main supporters on that occasion was the USSR, ironically an historic enemy of the Jewish people. Russia's ambassador to the UN, Andrei Gromyko, was known as 'Mr Nyet' for his frequent vetoing of American-sponsored motions in the General Assembly.

But for once, Russia and the United States were in agreement, not only with each other, but also with the eternal purposes of God!

The War of Independence

The third great miracle associated with the rebirth of Israel began on May 15th, 1948. The little State was less than one day old, yet found itself fighting for its life against powerful and deadly enemies.

The War of Independence officially began on November 30th, 1947 and continued throughout the next five and one-half months as the *Haganah* sought to take control of territory vacated by the withdrawing British forces.

During this time, the British Mandatory Government, whose policies and actions reflected the anti-semitic attitudes of Foreign Minister Ernest Bevin, did everything within its power short of open war to prevent the emergence of the State of Israel.

The British refused to abide by the UN resolution's requirement that the Mandatory Power evacuate a port (and surrounding area) for the reception of immigrants, and continued to adhere to the restrictions of the infamous 'White Paper' of 1939, which in effect, had condemned millions of European Jews to the gas chambers and ovens of Hitler's concentration camps by denying them access to the comparative safety of Palestine.

Displaced persons, without certificates of immigration, continued to be hunted, seized and deported to camps in Cyprus. Government stores, installations and essential records such as land registry deeds were either handed to the Arabs, destroyed, or conveniently 'lost'.

The Arabs switched from random raids and killings to increasingly focused attacks on Jewish settlements and vital roads, concentrating their efforts on isolating Jerusalem.

The British military forces openly tolerated – and even at times supported – the looting and murder carried out by armed bands of Arabs against Jews. They also used their military superiority to prevent the Jews from acquiring the weapons they needed to defend themselves.

The war, however, began in earnest on May 15th, 1948, when five Arab armies launched an invasion of Israel from every direction except the sea.

All in all, the war lasted for nearly sixteen months, consisted of close to forty military operations and involved mobilization of what amounted to the entire Jewish population of the Land (650,000), of which a staggering 1 per cent was killed.

The UN called for a month's ceasefire, beginning on June 11th. This lull in hostilities lasted for 28 days and changed the tide of the war.

The last stage of the war commenced in July, 1948, with a full-fledged, decisive and victorious Israeli offensive in which enemy forces were crushed, the danger to Tel Aviv eliminated, the siege of Jerusalem lifted, the Egyptians checked in the South, the Iraqis in the East, and the Syrians in the North. A second ceasefire halted the offensive.

On December 10th, 1948, the UN recognized the existence of

the State of Israel, and when armistices were signed with her enemies early in 1949, Israel was in possession of 23 per cent more territory than had been allocated to her by the 1947 Partition Plan!

There is no doubt but that Israel experienced Divine intervention on her behalf during the War of Independence.

Once again there was a *'sound of marching in the tops of the mulberry trees'* as the hosts of God waged war against the principalities and powers that were set to destroy the ancient covenant people.

Jewish officers discovered in the Bible a valuable military manual and drew inspiration from the exploits of Joshua, some 3,000 years before. As with Joshua, the Presence of God's miraculous power was the difference between victory and defeat.

During the early stages of the war, when the city of Jerusalem was being bombarded by the Arab Legion's field guns and her one hundred thousand inhabitants had almost exhausted their rations of food and water, it was the discovery of an ancient track that began somewhere near the Trappist Monastery of Latrun and disappeared into the Judean hills which helped to save the city from starvation and annihilation.

This shepherd's path to Jerusalem by-passed the Arab strong-point and became the vital alternative route to the besieged city. Convoys from Tel Aviv somehow managed to haul their loads of flour over this track which became known as 'Israel's Burma Road'. It was also the route that trucks, laden with arms and ammunition, used to re-equip the Israeli forces during the first ceasefire which began on June 11th.

Without it, and without that first invaluable 28 day truce, the fate of Jerusalem and the course of events in the Middle East might have been very different.

Other miraculous events occurred throughout the Land which helped change the direction of the war.

When the enemy was approaching Tel Aviv, it is reported that the bees fought for Israel. Swarms of these creatures from the groves east of Petach Tikvah, the oldest Jewish agricultural settlement, attacked the Arabs. Egyptian soldiers surrendered when they believed they were surrounded by a vast army. On another occasion, sickness immobilized a combined Syrian and Lebanese force in Galilee.

Affirmation of the Miraculous

The Presence of the Miraculous is God's way of attesting to the authenticity of an individual or a people. In this respect, Israel stands unique among the nations of the world.

What other nation has experienced the miraculous working of God on its behalf like Israel!

What other nation has seen its people taken captive, sold into slavery and dispersed among the nations of the world, only to be regathered thousands of years later and re-established as a sovereign power in its own land!

What other nation has experienced the death of its language, only to see it revived thousands of years later and once again become the language of the people!

What other nation has suffered the destruction of its cities and the desolation of its vineyards, only to see them rebuilt and replanted thousands of years later – often with the same names, in the same places!

What other nation has endured such persecution and reproach, such discrimination and rejection, only to see its captors and tormentors disappear into the abyss of oblivion while it continues to exist!

What other nation, when conquered and dispersed, has been able to resist the pressure of assimilation and successfully maintain its distinctive spiritual, cultural and racial identity!

Most assuredly, Israel is a miracle-in-the-making in the hand of the Lord!

Chapter 4

First the Natural, Then the Spiritual

*'However, the spiritual is not first, but the natural, and
afterward the spiritual.'*   (1 Corinthians 15:46)

The Word of God makes it abundantly clear that the natural
regathering and restoration of Israel will precede the spiritual
renewal of the Jewish people. Return to God's Land will precipitate reconciliation to God's Messiah.

In graphic terms, the Bible describes the regathering of the
exiles, the cultivation of the Land, and the rebuilding of the
cities:

*'Fear not, for I am with you; I will bring your descendants
from the east, and gather you from the west; I will say to the
north, "Give them up!" And to the south, "Do not keep
them back!" Bring My sons from afar, and My daughters
from the ends of the earth – Everyone who is called by My
name, whom I have created for My glory...'*

(Isaiah 43:5–7)

Please note that God is the prime-mover behind Israel's
regathering. God says, *'I will bring ... I will say ... I am with
you.'* The restoration of Zion is God's idea, not man's. And
God's power alone will bring it to pass!

It is also important to note that in regathering His people,
God uses different methods in different places.

God *brings* the descendants of Israel from the East (Asia) and *gathers* them from the West (the Americas).

But when it comes to dealing with the North and the South, God apparently encounters a certain reluctance on the part of these nations to allow the Jewish people to leave.

In the imperative tense, God says: *'Give them up ... Do not keep them back!'*

The land of the North can be readily identified as Russia and the satellite states of the former USSR. The 'South' denotes such countries as Yemen and Ethiopia (the original Hebrew word was *Teman* or *Yemen*).

In the last five years (1989–1993) we have witnessed significant ingatherings from these two regions, in accordance with God's Prophetic Word.

Hundreds of thousands of Soviet Jews took advantage of Mikhail Gorbachev's comparatively liberal emigration policy and made *Aliyah*, the peak year being 1990, in which 185,000 people immigrated to Israel from the 'land of the north'.

Likewise, in May, 1991, the majority of the Jewish population of Ethiopia was airlifted to Israel in a daring twenty-four hour rescue mission known as *Operation Solomon*.

Over 14,000 people (including eight babies born en route) were flown from Addis Ababa to their ancestral homeland in a complex operation that involved a total of forty sorties by IAF and EL AL planes – including a reported world record of 1,080 passengers on one Jumbo cargo flight!

In both cases, North and South, there were powerful spiritual forces at work, preventing the Jewish people from returning to the Promised Land.

The regathering of the exiles and the restoration of Zion is central to the fulfilment of God's prophetic purpose. Therefore it is violently opposed by the powers of darkness and the modern day 'Pharaohs' which rule in the spiritual realm over cities and nations.

The only weapon that can 'disarm kings and rulers' and 'break in pieces the gates of bronze', and thus release the Jewish people to return to Zion, is the Prophetic Word of God. This has proven true both in respect to the Communist regime of Ethiopian dictator Mengistu Haile Mariam and the citadel of darkness known as the Kremlin.

It is the weapon of God's Word, spoken thousands of years ago by His servants, and spoken again in faith and love by intercessors around the world, that binds the strong man and plunders his house!

The Process of Regathering

The process of regathering which began in the latter part of the Nineteenth Century, greatly increased in the 1930s as the shadow of Adolf Hitler fell upon Europe, and in particular, upon European Jewry.

As the horrors of war and Hitler's *Final Solution* engulfed Europe, the plight of the Jews became desperate. Of the almost nine million Jews in Europe, only a remnant escaped death.

The prophet Jeremiah accurately described, some 2,500 years ago, the events of the 1930s and the poignant regathering of the surviving remnant:

> '"Therefore behold, the days are coming," says the LORD, "that it shall no more be said, 'The LORD lives who brought up the children of Israel from the land of Egypt,' but, 'The LORD lives who brought up the children of Israel from the land of the north and from all the lands where He had driven them.' For I will bring them back into their land which I gave to their fathers. Behold, I will send for many fishermen," says the LORD, "and they will fish them; and afterward I will send for many hunters, and they shall hunt them from every mountain and every hill, and out of the holes of the rocks."'* (Jeremiah 16:14–16)

First of all, God sent the 'fishermen' – the Zionists. They sought to persuade the Jewish community to immigrate to Palestine and help build up the Jewish State, at the same time warning them of the consequences of remaining in Europe.

One must remember that European Jewry was a well-established community which, in some cases, was quite prosperous and influential.

51

Despite their not being allowed to completely assimilate, the Jews made significant contributions to the nations in which they lived. For example, up until World War Two, Jews accounted for one-third of all German Nobel Prize winners.

The Jewish community numbered among its ranks some of Europe's finest doctors, scientists, lawyers, musicians, artists, authors, and of course, tailors! By the late 1930s, the creativity and productivity of Polish Jewry (which, as a three million strong community accounted for one-third of Europe's Jews) was at a peak.

In light of this, it is easy to understand why so many were reluctant to exchange the rich heritage of life in Europe for a piece of real estate in the Middle East, which at that time was desolate and uninviting. In essence, it meant starting all over again.

Regretfully, the curse of materialism cost millions of people their lives as well as their possessions. It should be pointed out, however, that many did desire to leave Europe and immigrate to Palestine, but were prevented from doing so by the iniquitous immigration restrictions of the British Mandatory Government. (The White Paper of 1939 limited Jewish immigration to a total of 75,000, after which further immigration was subject to Arab approval.)

The Nazi seizure of Western Poland sent millions of Jews searching for escape and refuge, somewhere, anywhere. For the Jews of Palestine, these fugitives were not distant objects of pity, but parents, brothers, sisters, and friends who were doomed to destruction, whom they yearned to take in.

For this reason Britain is, to my mind, an accessory to the crime of the Holocaust. Her subsequent demise as a world power, the protracted war of attrition with the IRA, and the gradual 'Islamization' of her society are directly related to her handling of the Jewish people during that critical period of time.

Indeed, the nation or kingdom that refuses to cooperate with God's purpose for Israel will perish! (Isaiah 60:12).

Interestingly enough, the Hebrew word *'abad'*, translated 'perish', means 'to wander away' or 'lose oneself', and by implication, 'to perish' or 'come to destruction'. It bespeaks a process of deterioration, leading to eventual ruin.

This stands as a warning to any nation or denomination, religious or secular, that sets itself in opposition to God's purpose for Israel, as revealed in His Prophetic Word!

> *'Thus says the LORD: "The people who survived the sword found grace in the wilderness – Israel, when I went to give him rest ... the remnant of Israel ... behold I will bring them from the north country, and gather them from the ends of the earth, among them the blind and the lame, the woman with child and the one who labors with child together; a great throng shall return there. They shall come with weeping, and with supplications I will lead them. I will cause them to walk by the rivers of waters, in a straight way in which they shall not stumble; for I am a Father to Israel, and Ephraim is My firstborn."'* (Jeremiah 31:2, 7–9)

After the Zionist 'fishermen' came the Nazi 'hunters'. Those who managed to escape the horrors of the holocaust were literally driven out of Europe by Hitler's war machine.

Once again, Jeremiah's prophecy is so accurate, it could well serve as a 1940s newsreel commentary depicting survivors of the holocaust making their way to *Eretz* Israel – and to freedom!

In January, 1950, Jerusalem became the capital of Israel, and six months later the Knesset passed the Law of Return whereby any Jew had the right to immigrate to the Land.

This proclamation opened the flood gates and soon immigrants began arriving in airlifts at the rate of 1,000 per day from all over the world.

In the first eighteen months of statehood, over 340,000 Jews entered the Land – coming from 74 countries, speaking as many languages, representing all levels and all kinds of culture and development, and adhering to a myriad of customs.

Five thousand Jews even made *Aliyah* from China in fulfilment of Isaiah's prophecy concerning an ingathering from the land of *Sinnim* (Isaiah 49:12).

By the end of 1951 Israel had taken in, and unto herself, 764,900 immigrants, thereby more than doubling the population of the Jewish community in the Land.

The most famous people-movements were *Operation Ali Baba* which brought in over 100,000 Jews from Iraq, and *Operation Magic Carpet*, in which 48,000 Jews were airlifted from Yemen.

The Jews of Iraq were the oldest recorded Jewish community of the Diaspora, dating back to the Babylonian captivity. Significantly, they left Baghdad with only the clothes on their backs, vowing never to return.

For the persecuted and disadvantaged Jews of Yemen, the *Aliyah* was a dream come true. When news got through that there was 'a State in Israel', then that there was 'war in Israel', then that 'the proper hour had come' for them to return, people began to stream to Aden from 800 different points in the country.

Many of the Yemenite Jews had never seen a plane before, but there was no panic when the great airlift started. They believed they were *'mounting up with wings as eagles'*, as spoken by the prophet Isaiah (Isaiah 40:31). Carrying the Torah in their hands and the promise of Messiah in their hearts, they returned to the Land. God had indeed spoken to the South!

Significant changes were also taking place throughout the Land: some 200 new settlements were founded in the course of the State's first eighteen months. Thousands of acres of newly irrigated land helped to supply food for the burgeoning population. And using the Bible as a guide, teams of experts combed the Land (especially the Negev) for minerals, finding commercially useful copper, iron ore and manganese.

Further immigration took place during the 1950s with more Jews coming from Poland and Hungary. Between June 1967 and June 1975, a total of 103,000 Soviet Jews made *Aliyah*. And in 1985, in a venture known as *Operation Moses*, some 7,000 Ethiopian Jews were airlifted to Israel to join approximately the same number who had arrived in the country between 1980 and the Autumn of 1984.

Facing the Future

The miraculous advances of the last few years notwithstanding, the greatest *Aliyah* is still to come, both from the land of the north and the countries of the west!

The steady flow of immigrants from the Commonwealth of Independent States (formerly the USSR) and Eastern Europe could well develop into a floodtide of refugees, thereby necessitating the launching of a desperate rescue mission by the Jewish Agency and other likeminded organizations.

As of this writing, dedicated Christians are risking their lives to transport Jewish evacuees from the war-torn region of Trans-Dniester to Odessa, and on to Israel.

In some cases, Jews are literally being snatched off the street and taken into the comparative safety of Christian-sponsored buses amidst sniper fire and falling mortar shells!

The demise of Communism in Eastern Europe has been at once a blessing and a curse. It has led to unprecedented freedom of expression which, thanks be unto God, is being utilized for the preaching of the Gospel, but regretfully, is also being used for the promulgation of long suppressed nationalistic pride, religious bigotry, racial prejudice, and of course, **anti-semitism**.

Jews are once again being made scapegoats for Russia's economic and social ills and are being blamed for the Bolshevik Revolution and the failure of Communism.

Hundreds of thousands of Jews are desperately seeking to leave. It is no longer just a matter of improving one's economic status; it is quickly becoming a matter of survival!

Whether they come by airplane, bus or ship, or are forced to flee on foot, God will bring His people forth out of the land of the north. The *'Highway of Holiness'* spoken of by Isaiah the prophet is now being established in Scandinavia and Europe (Isaiah 35:8).

God is preparing Christian believers in these countries to receive and assist the Jews as they embark on the journey to Zion.

It is instructive to note the sequence of events which brought the Soviet Union to the point of releasing the Jews. Through a series of Divine judgments Russia and her confederate states were brought to their knees and forced, like Egypt of old, to 'cough up' the prisoners of Zion.

The Afghanistan war, Chernobyl, the Armenian earthquake, agricultural disasters, severe climatic changes, food shortages, a bankrupt economy, nationalist independence movements, and the overthrowing of Communism all contributed to the Soviet Union's demise.

And through it all God continues to say, *'Let My people go!'*

But what of the Jewish community in the West? What will it take to inspire the Jews of North America to make *Aliyah*? One thing is certain: As demonstrated in the Book of Exodus, God is able to make His people very willing, very quickly!

In his remarkable book *The Harvest*, Rick Joyner states:

> 'There will be a conflict in the Middle East that will result in Damascus being utterly destroyed. This will be done in such a way that the world will become enraged at Israel. Many of the problems then sweeping the world will be blamed on Jews who will have been holding key economic and political positions, seemingly indicating a conspiracy. Even the United States will wash its hands of Israel and participate in the new holocaust. Jews will be killed and driven out of every nation on earth.'[1]

If this is true, and I have no reason to doubt it, the very foundations of American-Jewish life will soon be shaken.

The pattern has already been established. In its 1990 *Audit of Anti-Semitic Incidents*, the Anti-Defamation League revealed that for the fourth year in a row, a record number of anti-semitic incidents was committed in the United States.

According to the report there has been a particularly dramatic rise in campus bigotry, with the number of anti-semitic incidents on campuses jumping by 72 percent in three years.

Harassment is at an all-time peak. Forms of harassment include assault and mail or phone threats, verbal abuse, physical violence, and acts of vandalism such as arson, bombings, cemetery desecrations and swastika daubings on Jewish owned and public property.

And according to a 1992 nationwide survey released by the Anti-Defamation League of *B'nai B'rith*, nearly forty million Americans – one out of every five adults – hold strongly anti-semitic views, and furthermore, ADL analysts said that today's anti-semitism has taken a 'dangerous turn' from social to polit-ical.

> '"In 1964, they said they didn't want to live with Jews, they didn't want to work with or marry Jews," said ADL dir-ector Abe Foxman. "Today, an ugly, more dangerous atti-tude of political rather than social anti-semitism has begun to take hold in the US, similar to that of Europe 30, 40, 50 years ago. An anti-semitism tied to the old canard of alleged Jewish power and control."'

This trend is not peculiar to the United States, but is indica-tive of a world-wide revival of anti-semitism, the ramifications of which are most clearly demonstrated in reunited Germany.

Even more significantly, 1992 saw a dramatic increase (by American standards) in Jewish *Aliyah* from the United States. The most frequently cited reasons were worsening economic conditions and increasing big city violence.

In order to understand what is presently happening and what is about to take place, one must appreciate the nature of the Heavenly Father, as described in Deuteronomy chapter thirty-two:

> *'For the LORD's portion is His people; Jacob is the place of His inheritance. He found him in a desert land and in the wasteland, a howling wilderness; He encircled him, He instructed him, He kept him as the apple of His eye. As an eagle stirs up its nest, hovers over its young, spreading out its wings, taking them up, carrying them on its wings, so the LORD alone led him, and there was no foreign god with him.'* (Deuteronomy 32:9–12)

God has made an eternal investment in His people; there-fore, He will go to any lengths to realize a profitable return from their lives.

'As an eagle stirs up its nest...' God will disturb the comfort and complacency of His people by whatever means necessary, in order to provoke them to do His will and fulfil His purpose. In this sense, persecution can be a tool in the hand of the Lord to galvanize His people to obedience.

God is determined to bring the Jews back from **all the countries** where He has scattered them, and if need be He will remove the silver lining from the social nest so as to induce them to 'get out of the briar and get on to the wing!'

The Lord is waiting patiently to lead His people home – yes, even to take them up and replant them in the Land of Israel.

Of this we can be certain: when the door to North America, France, Britain and Australia slams shut and the Jewish people are cast out, the door to Israel will open wider than ever before, beckoning them to their God-appointed destiny!

Fruitfulness in the Land

Meanwhile, the Prophetic Word of God continues to be fulfilled in the growth and development of the nation.

Israel has *'blossomed and budded'* and is *'filling the world with fruit'* (Isaiah 27:6). Choice Israeli citrus fruits are sold to hundreds of export markets around the world. During the 1980s, several new Israeli-developed tropical fruits successfully joined Israel's noted melons, strawberries and avocados on the world stage (and dining table).

Vineyards have been planted in various parts of the Land, with award winning and world famous wines being produced on the once barren Golan Heights. The desert continues to *'rejoice and blossom as the rose'* (Isaiah 35:1). Vast areas of wasted swampland and desolate wilderness have been reclaimed and lovingly transformed into fertile agricultural settlements.

Indeed, Israel is recognized as one of the most successful agricultural nations in the world, and one of the few countries on earth where the desert is actually receding!

Credit for these advances is undoubtedly due to the care and commitment of the Jewish people. However, there is another factor at work which ultimately is the most important element in the whole process of regathering and restoration:

> *'For the* LORD *will comfort Zion, He will comfort all her waste places; He will make her wilderness like Eden, and her desert like the garden of the* LORD; *joy and gladness will be found in it, thanksgiving and the voice of melody.'*
>
> (Isaiah 51:3)

It is the Presence and Blessing of the Lord that makes the difference. God has married the people to the Land and He is causing the Land to respond to their tender and passionate touch (Isaiah 62:4, 5).

During a ministry trip to Israel in 1969, American evangelist Oral Roberts had the privilege of meeting one of the world's most famous physicians and the discoverer of the cure for silicosis, **Dr Mann**, who, at the time, supervised the staff of the Hebrew University Hadassah Medical School.

> 'As I journeyed across Israel I was impressed with the health and general well-being of the Jewish people. Meeting one of the world's most famous physicians, I asked, "Dr Mann, how do you account for the good health of the Jewish people?" This eminent doctor smiled proudly as he replied, "Reverend Roberts, it is truly remarkable. As you know, these people came from everywhere. Once, more than 5,000 suffering from infectious tuberculosis were brought in at one time. I was truly frightened. I didn't know what to do. But the strangest thing took place. The very moment these people set foot on the soil of Israel, something happened inside them. They began to get well quickly. Our doctors and our nurses moved into their tents and worked with them, showering their love and attention upon them. The people responded. I almost believe they would have recovered without treatment. Today, we have only 800 bed patients in all of Israel with tuberculosis. My answer is, 'I believe God did it!'" '[2]

The People and the Land cannot be separated. They are bound together by an everlasting covenant (Genesis 17:8). The Land without the People will languish; the People without the Land will perish!

'*"Behold, the days are coming," says the* LORD, *"When the plowman shall overtake the reaper, and the treader of grapes him who sows seed; the mountains shall drip with sweet wine, and all the hills shall flow with it. I will bring back the captives of My people Israel; they shall build the waste cities and inhabit them; they shall plant vineyards and drink wine from them; they shall also make gardens and eat fruit from them. I will plant them in their land, and no longer shall they be pulled up from the land I have given them," says the* LORD *your God.'* (Amos 9:13–15)

The miracle of restoration is taking place in the Land. The exiles are returning, the cities are being rebuilt, vineyards are being planted, gardens are being established. However, the best is yet to come.

The wonderful transformation taking place in the natural realm is but a prelude to an even more remarkable transformation soon to occur in the spiritual realm!

References

1. *The Harvest* by Rick Joyner. Morningstar Publications, Pineville, NC, p. 138.
2. *God's Timetable for the End of Time*, by Oral Roberts. Heliotrope Publications, Tulsa, Oklahoma, pp. 36–7.

Chapter 5

The Redeemer Will Come to Zion

'"The Redeemer will come to Zion, and to those who turn from transgression in Jacob," says the LORD. "As for Me," says the LORD, "This is My covenant with them: My Spirit who is upon you, and My words which I have put in your mouth, shall not depart from your mouth, nor from the mouth of your descendants, nor from the mouth of your descendants' descendants," says the LORD, "from this time and forevermore. Arise, shine; for your light has come! And the glory of the LORD is risen upon you."'

(Isaiah 59:20, 21; 60:1)

In the latter part of 1989, the Lord gave me a key word for the Decade of the 90s, a word that defines His purpose for both Israel and the Church. The Word of the Lord was simply, *Visitation!*

The Bible abounds with examples of God's desire to visit His people. From the very beginning, when God walked and talked with Adam and Eve in the Garden of Eden, His intention was to *'dwell in them and walk among them, to be their God and for them to be His people'* (2 Corinthians 6:16). Union and communion between God and man represents the heart of His eternal purpose.

In order to properly understand the heart of God toward Israel, or indeed, the heart of the Lord Jesus toward His Church, one should think in terms of the affection and love of a bridegroom for his bride, or the devotion of a husband to his wife.

Throughout the prophetic writings, the heart of God grieved over the failings and faithlessness of His bride. Because of her multiplied acts of spiritual adultery and her incorrigible sinfulness, God was forced to put her away, albeit temporarily, thereby giving her over to judgment, which most always took the form of foreign incursion and occupation.

Israel's unbelief and disobedience reached a climax with her rejection of Jesus the Messiah, the promised Deliverer of Israel and the Saviour of all men. *'He came unto His own, and His own did not receive Him ... He was despised and rejected by men ... the Stone which the builders rejected has become the chief Cornerstone...'*

For Israel, the cost of rejecting her Messiah was enormous. It resulted in generations of incalculable suffering and heartache. Jesus Himself wept over Jerusalem when He foresaw the inevitable consequences of her spiritual blindness and hardness of heart.

As He drew near, He saw the city and wept over it, saying,

> *'"If you had known, even you, especially in this your day, the things that make for your peace! But now they are hidden from your eyes. For the days will come upon you when your enemies will build an embankment around you, surround you and close you in on every side, and level you, and your children within you to the ground; and they will not leave in you one stone upon another, because you did not know the time of your visitation."'*   (Luke 19:41–44)

Later, as He sat on the Mount of Olives with His disciples and gazed down on the splendour of Herod's temple, Jesus said:

> *'"As for these things which you see, the days will come in which not one stone shall be left upon another that shall not be thrown down ... but when you see Jerusalem surrounded by armies, then know that its desolation is near. Then let*

those in Judea flee to the mountains, let those who are in the midst of her depart, and let not those who are in the country enter her. For these are the days of vengeance, that all things which are written may be fulfilled. But woe to those who are pregnant and to those who are nursing babies in those days! For there will be great distress in the land and wrath upon this people. And they will fall by the edge of the sword, and be led away captive into all nations. And Jerusalem will be trampled by Gentiles until the times of the Gentiles are fulfilled."'   (Luke 21:6, 20–24)

Some forty years later, Jesus' terrible prophecy was fulfilled, word for word, by the forces of the Roman Empire. The Holy City had already received two reprieves. The Roman Procurator in Syria, Cestius Gallus, withdrew suddenly in October of AD 67 when the City was his for the taking. Nine months later, Vespasian, upon hearing of Nero's death, halted his march on Jerusalem and returned to Rome to eventually be crowned as Emperor.

During the next eighteen months, those who remembered the words of Jesus fled from the City and took refuge in Pella, east of the Jordan river.

But the reprieve was short-lived, the siege was resumed, and on May 10th, AD 70, the shadow of Titus, Vespasian's son, fell across the walls of Jerusalem. It took Titus' army of sixty-five thousand men a total of 139 days to gain control of the city, and during that time it was spared no form of savagery or horror.

Over one million people had come up to Jerusalem for the Feast of Unleavened Bread, only to find themselves shut up within the walls by the Roman siege.

Those who did not die at the hands of rival Jewish factions starved to death by the thousands. Others who tried to escape were captured by the Romans and executed. At one stage five hundred Jews were crucified daily within sight of those on the walls, until there was no more room to erect crosses and no more wood could be found for bodies.

Finally, on the 10th day of Ab, AD 70 (the very same day on which Solomon's temple had been destroyed by the King of

Babylon in 586 BC), the temple was set on fire and destroyed (contrary to Titus' orders) by Roman soldiers.

Overall, some two million Jews perished in the seven year revolt against Rome, and a further one million were taken prisoner and sold as slaves.

And so began the long night of the Second Jewish Diaspora. The cry of the chief priests, *'We have no king but Caesar ... His blood be on us and on our children'* signalled the beginning of Gentile domination of the Jewish people and their Promised Land.

Judgment Gives Way to Mercy

When God judges His people, He always has a redemptive purpose in mind. Like a faithful father who disciplines his aberrant children, God chastens us that we may not be condemned with the world, but rather, may be partakers of His holiness.

God's chastening of Israel has as its ultimate goal, the redemption and reconciliation of the Ancient Covenant People.

> *'"Do not fear, for you will not be ashamed; neither be disgraced, for you will not be put to shame; for you will forget the shame of your youth, and will not remember the reproach of your widowhood anymore. For your Maker is your husband, the LORD of hosts is His name; and your Redeemer is the Holy One of Israel; He is called the God of the whole earth. For the LORD has called you like a woman forsaken and grieved in spirit, like a youthful wife when you were refused," says your God. "For a mere moment I have forsaken you, but with great mercies I will gather you. With a little wrath I hid My face from you for a moment; but with everlasting kindness I will have mercy on you," says the LORD, your Redeemer.'* (Isaiah 54:4–8)

Like many prophetic Scriptures, these verses are capable of at least four interpretations and applications.

Firstly, they bear undeniable reference to Jerusalem's restoration under the Persian king, Darius the Great. However, this creates a dilemma because some of the language in the prophecy is clearly Messianic and eschatological, and was at best, fulfilled in a partial or precursory manner under the reign of Darius.

Secondly, the New Testament Apostles interpreted these verses (and others like them) as referring to Messiah and His Church (see Galatians 4:27).

Thirdly, these verses may be interpreted as referring to the end-time restoration of national Israel, consistent with Jesus' statement in Luke 21:24 and Paul's teaching in Romans 11.

Fourthly, such prophetic passages may be seen as referring **in an ultimate sense** to the age to come, and thus, will be completely realized under Messiah's glorious and universal reign.

Various interpretations notwithstanding, an objective reading of passages like Isaiah 54 yields prophetic glimpses of the end-time regathering of the Jewish people and rebirth of the Jewish nation.

For a mere moment God forsook them and hid His face from them – but now, with great mercies and everlasting kindness, God is gathering the dispersed ones to Himself.

However, history bears tragic testimony to the fact that religious doctrine and tradition is very often inconsistent with the Word and character of God.

Since the time of the Fourth Century the Christian Church has been beset by a false theology which declares that God is angry with Israel and is exacting a toll from 'the wandering Jews' for rejecting the Lord Jesus.

Indeed, some of the most terrible anti-semitic declarations on record have been made by Christian preachers such as the Fourth Century church father **John Chrysostom** and the Sixteenth Century reformer **Martin Luther**.

The disposition of God toward Israel, in contradistinction to the attitude of men, even good religious men, is one of grace, mercy and love. He longs to pour His Spirit upon them and give them a new heart; He yearns to cleanse them from sin and reconcile them to Himself in the righteousness of faith.

'And they also, if they do not continue in unbelief, will be grafted in, for God is able to graft them in again. For if you were cut out of the olive tree which is wild by nature, and were grafted contrary to nature into a good olive tree, how much more will these, who are the natural branches, be grafted into their own olive tree? Concerning the Gospel they are enemies for your sakes, but concerning the election they are beloved for the sake of the fathers. For the gifts and the calling of God are irrevocable.'

(Romans 11:23–24, 28–29)

In the eyes of God, the Jewish people are **beloved** – for the sake of the fathers. The Lord is ever mindful of His covenant with Abraham, Isaac and Jacob. In spite of her unbelief and disobedience, Israel continues to be the *'apple of God's eye'* – the focus of His love and attention.

The word 'beloved' comes from the Greek verb *'agapao'* (to love), and describes God's attitude toward both the Church and Israel.

'It expresses the deep and constant love and interest of a Perfect Being towards entirely unworthy objects, producing and fostering a reverential love in them towards the Giver, and a practical love towards those who are partakers of the same, and a desire to help others to seek the Giver.'[1]

Has Israel's contrariness to the Gospel abrogated its uniqueness as a covenant people in the purposes of God? The Apostle Paul deals with this question at length in Romans nine through eleven. And in his own inimitable way, Paul shows that Israel's rejection is neither total nor final.

For example, Paul (quoting the prophet Isaiah) reproves Israel for her unbelief and disobedience in one breath, and then refers to them as *'God's people'* in the next! (Romans 10:21; 11:1)

And in the opening verse of chapter eleven, Paul asks the rhetorical question: *'Has God cast away His people?'* The question is so phrased in the Greek text that it requires a negative answer: **'Certainly not!'** or *'God forbid!'* Paul uses precisely the same phrase in Romans 6:2 with regard to Christians continuing in sin: 'May it never occur,' or 'Perish the thought!'

The Greek word *'apotheo'*, translated 'cast away', means 'to thrust or drive away from one's self', 'repel', 'repudiate'. But Paul states quite categorically that *'God has not cast away His people whom He foreknew!'*

Foreknowledge issues in election and election issues in covenant. A Divine repudiation of Israel would effectively mean a breaking of covenant, which would be tantamount to the self-repudiation of God Himself.

God has not rejected Israel totally for *'at this present time there is a remnant according to the election of grace,'* which remnant is growing day by day!

And God has not rejected Israel finally for *'have they stumbled that they should fall (irremediably and thus never rise again)? Certainly not!'*

Though they have fallen, yet shall they rise again in newness of life. Though they have been cast away, yet shall they be accepted. Though they have been broken off, yet shall they be grafted in. Though they have been diminished, yet shall they be made complete!

Dr Henry Alford makes the following observation in *Alford's Greek Testament*:

> 'But a question even more important arises, not unconnected with that just discussed: namely, Who are "His people"? In order for the sentence "For I also am etc.", to bear the meaning just assigned to it, it is obvious that "His people" must mean the people of God *nationally* considered. If Paul deprecated such a proposition as the rejection of *God's people*, because he himself would thus be *as an Israelite* cut off from God's favour, the rejection assumed in the hypothesis must be a *national rejection*.
>
> 'It is against *this* that he puts in his strong protest. It is *this* which he disproves by a cogent historical parallel from Scripture, showing that there is a remnant even at this present time according to the election of grace: and not

only so, but that that part of Israel (considered as having continuity of national existence) which is for a time hardened, shall ultimately come in, and so all Israel (nationally considered again, Israel *as a nation*) shall be saved.

'Thus the covenant of God with Israel, having been *national*, shall ultimately be fulfilled to them as a *nation*: not by the gathering in merely of *individual* Jews, or of *all* the Jews individually, into the Christian Church, – but by the *national restoration* of the Jews, not in unbelief, but as a *Christian believing nation, to all that can, under the gospel, represent their ancient pre-eminence*, and to the fulness of those promises which have *never yet in their plain sense been accomplished to them.*'[2]

Having temporarily set them aside, God is once again stretching forth His hand to His ancient covenant people. His purpose is to graft them back into the Olive Tree – to make them partakers of His promise in Messiah, fellow heirs together with believing Gentiles, and members of the eternal Body-Bride of His Son!

An impossible task? For man, yes. But with God, all things are possible. God is able to graft them in again. God is able to remove the veil from their eyes. God is able to pour out His Spirit upon them and give them a heart of faith!

The Road to Damascus

The nation of Israel is involved in a spiritual journey known as 'the road to Damascus'. This designation comes from the life of Rabbi Saul (later called the Apostle Paul), who

'. . . *breathing threats and murder against the disciples of the Lord, went to the high priest and asked letters from him to the synagogues of Damascus, so that if he found any who were of the Way, whether men or women, he might bring them bound to Jerusalem. As he journeyed he came near Damascus, and suddenly a light shone around him from heaven. Then he fell to the ground, and heard a voice saying to him, "Saul, Saul, why are you persecuting Me?" And he said, "Who are You, Lord?" Then the Lord said, "I am Jesus, whom you are persecuting. It is hard for you to kick against the goads." So he, trembling and astonished, said, "Lord, what do You want me to do?" Then the Lord said to him, "Arise and go into the city, and you will be told what you must do."'* (Acts 9:1–6)

When Saul commenced this journey he had no intention of 'getting saved'. Indeed, his faith in *Yeshua HaMashiach* was the direct result of a sovereign encounter and a supernatural revelation! Suddenly a great light from heaven shone around Saul, and a voice spoke, calling him by name.

Nothing short of dramatic Divine intervention could have changed Saul from an ardent persecutor of the Way into an equally zealous Christian missionary.

But the question remains: Why did God intercede in Saul's life in such a sovereign and supernatural manner? The answer is found in Acts 9:15;

'But the Lord said to him, "Go, for he is a chosen vessel of Mine to bear My Name before Gentiles, kings, and the children of Israel."'

Saul was chosen by God before the foundation of the world and predestined according to His eternal purpose in Messiah Jesus. And in the fulness of time, when it pleased the Lord, He moved in on Saul and gave him a revelation of Jesus, and through that revelation gained control of his life.

Years later Saul (Paul) recounted his salvation experience in these words:

'... the Gospel which was preached by me ... came through the revelation of Jesus Christ. But when it pleased God, who separated me from my mother's womb and called me through His grace, to reveal His Son in me, that I might preach Him among the Gentiles ...'
(Galatians 1:11–12, 15–16)

Moreover, in his letter to the Philippians Paul speaks of the purpose *'for which Christ Jesus has also laid hold of me'* (Philippians 3:12). The Greek word *'katalambano'*, translated 'lay hold of' means 'to seize, lay hold of, and overcome'. The picture is of a football player who catches hold of his opponent and pulls him to the ground.

Messiah seized Saul on the road to Damascus, and (quite literally) pulled him to the ground and claimed him as His own!

Paul described himself as *'one born out of due time'* (1 Corinthians 15:8), an expression that refers both to his call in relation to the other apostles and to his rebirth in relation to the nation of Israel.

For what God did in the life of one man – a Hebrew of the Hebrews – on the road to Damascus, He will surely do in the life of a nation!

Just as Saul, a vehement adversary of the Way, became one of the major instruments for the spreading of the Gospel of the Kingdom in the First Century, so Israel, by the grace of God, will become one of the major instruments for the manifestation of God's Kingdom in the Last Century.

The conviction of Who Jesus is will come to Israel, even as it did to Saul, through a supernatural revelation of the Holy Spirit. John the Baptist said, *'I did not know Him* (Jesus)*; but that He should be revealed to Israel...'* (John 1:31).

Israel could only know Him then, and can only know Him now, through a revelation of the Holy Spirit. Indeed, *'the people who walk in darkness will see a great light; and those who dwell in the land of the shadow of death, upon them the light will shine'* (Isaiah 9:2).

The light of the revelation of Jesus will be overwhelming in its intensity; in a flash of revelation, God will destroy the proud and lofty arguments of men and humble the hearts of His people.

Just as Saul spent three days praying and fasting and humbling himself before the feet of his newly-revealed Lord, so Israel, in looking on Him whom they pierced, will mourn and grieve and overflow with grace and supplication, family by family and household by household throughout the length and breadth of the Land (Zechariah 12:10–14).

Human reasoning and theological debate will not convince the Jews that Jesus is the long-awaited Messiah, the Hope of Israel, but the revelation of the Holy Spirit, together with the faithful witness of sensitive believers will!

The Arm of the Lord will be revealed, and the knowledge of God's Holy One will fill the Land, and *'all the House of Israel will know assuredly that God has made this Jesus, who was crucified, both Lord and Messiah!'* (Acts 2:36).

Joseph and His Brothers

Joseph, the favoured seventh son of Jacob and the firstborn of his union with Rachel, is an Old Testament type of the Lord Jesus.

Like Joseph, our Lord was envied, misunderstood and rejected by His brethren. Like Joseph, He was betrayed and sold into the hands of the Gentiles. And like Joseph, He has been hidden from the sight of His brethren for 'twenty years' (twenty centuries), during which time He has been received by many of the Gentiles and hailed as Saviour and King.

Joseph's brethren finally came to him, albeit without perceiving his true identity, to buy grain in a time of severe famine. Thus, the pressure of need compelled them to fulfil Divine destiny.

And such shall be the case with the end-time nation of Israel. In their distress the Jewish people will cry to the Lord, and He will reveal Himself to them (Psalm 120:1). Israel will turn to the Lord out of great need, proving once again that man's extremity is God's opportunity!

The poignancy of reconciliation is revealed in the following verses:

> *'So Joseph recognized his brothers, but they did not recog-*
> *nize him. Then they said to one another, "We are truly*
> *guilty concerning our brother, for we saw the anguish of his*
> *soul when he pleaded with us, and we would not hear;*
> *therefore this distress has come upon us." And Reuben*

answered them, saying, "Did I not speak to you, saying,
'Do not sin against the boy'; and you would not listen?
Therefore behold, his blood is now required of us." But
they did not know that Joseph understood them, for he
spoke to them through an interpreter. And he turned himself
away from them and wept..."   (Genesis 42:8, 21–24a)

The Lord Jesus recognizes His brethren after the flesh,
indeed, He gazes upon them with longing eyes and yearning
heart, even though many of them do not yet know Him. He
who once wept in the flesh over Jerusalem now weeps in the
Spirit and makes intercession before the Throne of God.

Some readers have no doubt visited or at least seen pictures
of the Western Wall in Jerusalem's Old City. The *Kotel* is the
last surviving link with the Second Temple, and as such, is
considered by many Jews to be the holiest place on earth.

The plaza in front of the Wall is a popular venue for the
offering up of prayers, the chanting of psalms, and the reading
of the Torah. On high holy days the plaza is often filled with
tens of thousands of worshippers, gathered as it were in the
Presence of the Lord God of Israel.

A close friend of ours who leads a praise and worship ministry in Jerusalem had a vision in which she saw the Jewish people
standing before the Wall like the *Shulamite* in the Song of
Songs, and the Lord Jesus, *the Beloved*, standing behind the
Wall and gazing upon His fair one, as it were, through the
'lattice' (Song of Songs 2:9–14).

What is the Lord's attitude toward His brethren after the
flesh as He watches them return to the Land of Promise and go
about the business of building up Zion, still as touching the
Gospel, in blindness, ignorance and hardness of heart?

The following extract from the story of Joseph and his
brothers says it all:

'Then he lifted his eyes and saw his brother Benjamin, his
mother's son, and said, "Is this your younger brother of
whom you spoke to me?" And he said, "God be gracious to
you, my son." Now his heart yearned for his brother; so

> *Joseph made haste and sought somewhere to weep. And he
> went into his chamber and wept there.'*
>
> (Genesis 43:29, 30)

The Lord Jesus yearns for reconciliation with His brethren
after the flesh. Intercessors, mark well: the effectiveness of
one's prayer life is commensurate with the yearning of one's
heart. *'The effective, fervent prayer of a righteous man avails
much ... Elijah prayed earnestly... '* (James 5:16, 17)

The Apostle Paul declared that effective prayer for Israel is
the result of sharing the Lord's burden for reconciliation with
His people: *'Brethren, my heart's desire and prayer to God for
Israel is that they may be saved'* (Romans 10:1).

The Hebrew word *'kamar'*, translated 'yearn' in Genesis
43:30, has as its root meanings 'to be warm or hot', and 'to
intertwine or contract'. Figuratively it means 'to be deeply
affected with passion, love or pity'.

The Lord uses the same word when addressing wayward
Israel in Hosea 11:8;

> *'How can I give you up, Ephraim? How can I hand you
> over, Israel? How can I make you like Admah? How can I
> set you like Zeboim? My heart churns within Me; My sym-
> pathy is stirred.'*

The heart of the Lord constricts with passion as He gazes
upon His beloved people, their weakness and waywardness
notwithstanding. Divine affection is stirred and heavenly compassion is kindled.

O, that God would grant us a revelation of His heart toward
Israel! O, that God would raise up intercessors to pray in the
Spirit of Grace and Mercy!

The words of Joseph to his younger brother Benjamin aptly
express the attitude of Jesus toward His brethren after the flesh:
'God be gracious to you, my son!'

The Hebrew word *'chanan'*, translated 'gracious', means 'to
be graciously inclined toward someone'; 'to have compassion
on someone', and 'to bestow favour on a person in need'. The

attitude of graciousness is marked by 'compassion, generosity, and kindness'.

A derivative of this word is found in Zechariah 12:10, in which instance God declares that He will *'pour on the house of David and the inhabitants of Jerusalem the Spirit of grace and supplication.'*

God is graciously inclined toward His ancient covenant people – of this we can be sure. Up until now, however, His grace has been extended by measure – a blessing here and a favour there.

But the day is coming when the Lord Jesus will not be able to restrain Himself any longer; He will arise and *pour* His grace on the house of David and the inhabitants of Jerusalem – *lavishly!*

The soul of the priests will be filled to the full with God's abundance, and His people will be satisfied – abundantly supplied – with His goodness! (Jeremiah 31:14)

The Lord will send grain, new wine and oil (spiritual and material blessings) and His people will eat in plenty and be satisfied, and will praise the Name of the Lord their God for dealing wondrously with them! (Joel 2:19, 26)

> *'Then Joseph could not restrain himself before all those who stood by him, and he cried out, "Make everyone go out from me!" So no one stood with him while Joseph made himself known to his brothers. And he wept aloud ... and Joseph said to his brothers, "Please come near to me." So they came near. Then he said: "I am Joseph your brother, whom you sold into Egypt. But now, do not therefore be grieved or angry with yourselves because you sold me here; for God sent me before you to preserve life ... and God sent me before you to preserve a posterity for you in the earth, and to save your lives by a great deliverance."'*
>
> (Genesis 45:1–2a, 4–5, 7)

The reconciliation of Israel to the Lord must, of necessity, be the work of God and not man. Whilst God uses human instrumentality to accomplish His purposes, there comes a time when 'everyone must leave the room', so that God may deal with His people alone.

Because of the Jewish people's disobedience, God has veiled their eyes and blinded their vision – and only God can remove the veil and grant them clear collective sight.

But O, what a day of joy and rejoicing it will be for Gentiles who trust in Messiah Jesus when Israel's spiritual captivity is turned and she is grafted into the Vine!

In that day Israel will see that God used their fall to bring the riches of salvation to the Gentiles. And in that day the Gentiles will see that God used Israel's acceptance and fulness to consummate the whole plan of redemption, and to usher in the resurrection of the dead and the very return of the Lord!

And in that day believing Jews and Gentiles will raise one voice in an anthem of praise: *'Oh, the depth of the riches both of the wisdom and knowledge of God! How unsearchable are His judgments and His ways past finding out!'* (Romans 11:33).

Prophetic Pictures of Restoration

The prophet Zechariah paints a graphic picture of the outpouring of the Holy Spirit on the Jewish people in the last days:

> *"'And I will pour on the house of David and on the inhabitants of Jerusalem the Spirit of Grace and Supplication; then they will look on Me whom they have pierced; they will mourn for Him as one mourns for his only son, and grieve for Him as one grieves for a firstborn. In that day there shall be a great mourning in Jerusalem, like the mourning at Hadad Rimmon in the plain of Megiddo ... and the land shall mourn, every family by itself...*
>
> *"In that day a fountain shall be opened for the house of David and for the inhabitants of Jerusalem, for sin and for uncleanness. It shall be in the day," says the* LORD *of hosts, "that I will cut off the names of the idols from the land, and they shall no longer be remembered. I will also cause the prophets and the unclean spirit to depart from the land."'*
>
> (Zechariah 12:10–12a; 13:1–2)

It behoves us to note the natural and logical sequence of events, here described in the prophecy of Zechariah.

The primary factor in the restoration of Zion is **the will of God!** The Lord says, '*I will pour on the house of David ... the Spirit...*'

Whilst salvation involves an element of human decision and responsibility, the fact remains that one cannot approach God on his or her own initiative. This is as true of Jews as it is of Gentiles. Repentance is a gift of God (2 Timothy 2:25). No one can come to the Lord Jesus unless the Father draws him (John 6:44).

Christians need to be filled with the knowledge of God's will with regard to Jews as individuals, and Israel as a nation. The Word of God is the revelation of the will of God – the blueprint of all His plans and purposes.

The Word reveals the salvation of Israel to be the unalterable will and pleasure of the Lord. God Himself has purposed and promised to save His people, which fact guarantees its fulfilment!

Secondly, the nature of the outpouring of the Spirit and the subsequent disposition that it produces in the hearts of the Jewish people is **grace** and **supplication**.

The Holy Spirit is called *the Spirit of Grace* (Hebrews 10:29). His ministry of Grace is to convict of sin, righteousness and judgment, to guide into all truth, and to reveal the majesty of Jesus the Messiah (John 16:8–14). Without this ministry of Grace, one could not be saved!

The salvation of Israel is a sovereign work of God, accomplished through the outpouring of the Holy Spirit and His ministry of Grace. God will give the Jewish people a Spirit of wisdom and revelation in the knowledge of Him; the eyes of their understanding will be enlightened and they will '*look on Him who they have pierced.*'

Traditional eschatology, at least in my generation, has tended to relegate this particular prophecy to the 'Second Coming Basket'. However, I believe that such an interpretation is Scripturally unviable, and moreover, does despite to the redemptive ability of the Spirit of Grace.

Observant scholars will note that there is no explicit reference in Zechariah chapter twelve to the physical, visible return of the Lord Jesus. In fact, Messiah's return is not spoken of until chapter fourteen and verse three; *'Then the LORD will go forth and fight against those nations, as He fights in the day of battle. And in that day His feet will stand on the Mount of Olives, which faces Jerusalem on the east...'*

The spiritual eyes of the Jewish people are blinded, not their physical eyes. And it is with their spiritual eyes that they will *'look on Him whom they pierced,'* as did Saul on the road to Damascus, and as did you and I when we first heard the Gospel and received a revelation of the Saviour.

Recognition of Messiah will give way to yearning, and yearning will give way to entreaty. The Spirit's ministry of Grace will kindle a desire and a yearning, even a *compassion and a graciousness* in the hearts of the Jewish people toward *Yeshua,* their Redeemer.

This, in turn, will overflow in *supplications* – earnest, heartfelt entreaty and fervent, unceasing prayer!

Praying, like repenting, cannot be done in one's own strength or on one's own initiative. The Holy Spirit comes to our aid as we struggle with human weakness and inadequacy. He gives us the desire and ability to pray, to humble ourselves before God, and to repent of our sins. He makes intercession for us and through us with groanings which cannot be uttered (Romans 8:26).

The third aspect of the restoration of Zion, as portrayed by the prophet Zechariah, is **spontaneous nationwide repentance**. The realization of who Jesus is and what He has done will result in a massive outpouring of Godly sorrow.

Godly sorrow produces repentance, and repentance leads to salvation (2 Corinthians 7:10). The outpouring of mourning and grief that will accompany the revelation of Messiah is likened to the grief of a family at the death of a firstborn and only son.

In Jewish society, the firstborn son occupies a unique and privileged position. Therefore, the death of the firstborn is a terrible tragedy and a cause of great sorrow for both family and friends. Thus, the prophet seeks to convey the acuteness of Israel's grief and the depth of her sorrow as she considers the sacrificial death of God's only begotten Son, the 'Firstborn' among many brethren.

The prophet further compares the mourning that will take place in Jerusalem to that of Judah when King Josiah was slain in battle by Necho, King of Egypt. On that occasion, 'all Judah and Jerusalem' mourned for the King. There was an unprecedented outpouring of national grief. Prophets and singers together lamented the death of this Godly and righteous leader (2 Chronicles 35:20–25).

Whilst there will be a national expression of sorrow and repentance, the 'God of all the families of Israel' will deal with each family on an individual and personal level – *every family by itself*. From David to Nathan (representing the highest and the lowest of the royal order), and from Levi to Shimei (representing the highest and the lowest of the priestly order) – the Spirit of God will be poured out on all flesh!

Fourthly, a fountain will be opened for sin and uncleanness. The Jewish people will be introduced to the **the efficacy of the Blood of Jesus**, the Blood of the New Covenant, shed for many for the remission of sins.

'Sin' represents judicial guilt; 'Uncleanness' speaks of moral impurity. Thus, both justification and sanctification are provided in the Blood of Messiah, who put away sin by the sacrifice of Himself, and is Himself our righteousness and holiness.

What the blood of bulls and goats could only foreshadow but never accomplish, the Lord Jesus did, when He entered the Most Holy Place with His own blood, having obtained eternal redemption.

As the Spirit of Grace and Supplication falls on the Jewish people and they begin to call upon the Lord, the inherent power of the Blood of Messiah will be released in their lives, and they will enter into the redemption that was purchased on the Cross almost two thousand years ago!

A Very Heavy Stone

The above-quoted scenario of revival and restoration is a thrilling stimulus to believing prayer. However, one should not lose sight of the context of this great outpouring.

In verse two of Zechariah chapter twelve, the Lord declares

that He will *'make Jerusalem a cup of drunkenness or reeling to all the surrounding peoples, when they lay siege against Judah and Jerusalem.'* And moreover,

> *'It shall happen in that day that I will make Jerusalem a very heavy stone for all peoples; all who would heave it away will surely be cut in pieces, though all nations of the earth are gathered against it. It shall be in that day that I will seek to destroy all the nations that come against Jerusalem.'*
>
> (Zechariah 12:3, 9)

First of all, God speaks of a siege being laid against Judah and Jerusalem by all the *surrounding peoples*. One only has to look at a map of the Middle East to determine the identity of the 'surrounding peoples'. Israel is surrounded on all sides by Arab nations, who for the most part, are followers of the 'prophet' Mohammed and the religion of *Islam*.

The siege of which Zechariah speaks could very well be an *Islamic Jihad* – a final concerted attempt to destroy the Jewish State and turn the Middle East into a pan-Arab Islamic nation.

However, the issue of Jerusalem will not just concern the nations of the Middle East; it will ultimately solicit the involvement of every nation and government on the face of the earth!

The existence of Israel and the administration of Jerusalem will be **the international issue** of the last days. According to the Prophetic Word, *all peoples and all nations* will feel obliged to solve the age-old *'Jewish problem'*.

Some will try to *'heave Jerusalem away'*, that is, change its status and wrest control of the city from the hands of the Jewish people, either by military force or political pressure.

In the end, *all nations of the earth* will be *gathered against* Jewish Jerusalem, which in modern parlance would indicate international censure, political isolation, economic sanctions, land, sea and air blockades, and as a last resort, military confrontation.

But God promises to defend the inhabitants of Jerusalem and to personally destroy all the nations that come against her. Indeed, any nation, be it great or small, developing entity or established superpower, that opposes God's purpose in Jerusalem and Israel, will be cut in pieces!

It is in this context and against this background that God pledges to pour His Spirit out on the house of David and the inhabitants of Jerusalem.

Israel will find herself forced into a corner, with her back against the wall. In all of His dealings with Israel, God has one purpose in mind: *to get her attention!* Psalm 123:1, 2 puts it this way:

> *'Unto You I lift up my eyes, O You who dwell in the heavens. Behold, as the eyes of servants look to the hand of their masters, as the eyes of a maid to the hand of her mistress, so our eyes look to the LORD our God, until He has mercy on us.'*

The purpose of fiery trials is to produce unfeigned faith (1 Peter 1:6, 7). The dealings of God are designed to bring Israel to a point of trusting wholly in the Lord.

When she has no friends left among the governments of the world and she can no longer trust in the arm of flesh, God will have Israel right where He wants her – in a place of 'vulnerability' where her only hope is in the Name of the Lord!

God is working to bring Israel to the point of faith described in Psalm 124:

> *'"If it had not been the LORD who was on our side," let Israel now say – "If it had not been the LORD who was on our side, when men rose up against us..." Blessed be the LORD, Who has not given us as prey to their teeth. Our soul has escaped as a bird from the snare of the fowlers; the snare is broken, and we have escaped. Our help is in the name of the LORD, Who made heaven and earth.'*

With full face and open heart Israel will turn to the Lord. In the fulness of time, when world events and national circumstances have prepared the way for the movement of God's Spirit, Israel will seek the face of her Redeemer. And with great joy and rejoicing, He will be found of her!

An Appointment with God

The prophet Ezekiel also foretold the return of the Jewish people to *Eretz* Israel in the last days, and heralded it as a prelude to the greater miracle of spiritual renewal.

> '*For I will take you from among the nations, gather you out of all countries, and bring you into your own land. Then I will sprinkle clean water on you, and you shall be clean; I will cleanse you from all your filthiness and from all your idols. I will give you a new heart and put a new spirit within you; I will take the heart of stone out of your flesh and give you a heart of flesh. I will put My Spirit within you and cause you to walk in My statutes, and you will keep My judgments and do them. Then you shall dwell in the land that I gave to your fathers; you shall be My people, and I will be your God. I will deliver you from all your uncleannesses...*'
> (Ezekiel 36:24–29a)

Ezekiel states quite explicitly that the physical return of the people to the Land will precipitate the spiritual restoration of the people to the Lord. In the order of God's dealings, returning to the Land is a prerequisite to returning to the Lord!

God has promised to reveal Himself to His people in *Eretz* Israel – not in New York, St. Petersburg, or London. Which is not to say that God cannot reveal Himself to individuals in such places, for 'all over the world the Spirit is moving' upon Jew and Gentile alike.

Spiritual restoration, however, on the scale spoken of by the prophets, can only take place *in the Land*. This piece of real estate which the Lord variously refers to in the Scriptures as '*My Land*', or speaking of the Jewish people, '*Their Land*', is the appointed meeting place of God and Israel. There God will deal with her, cleanse her, and restore her to Himself.

Kibbutz Gaulioth (the ingathering of the exiles) is an integral part of God's purpose for the Jewish people. One can only wonder what God will do to disturb the comfort and complacency of Jews in North America and other Western nations, in order to provoke them to return to Israel!

Of this we can be certain: God has an appointment to keep with His beloved Israel, and the encounter is scheduled to take place **in their land!**

Once again, it is worthy to note the sequence of God's dealings with Israel, as described by the prophet Ezekiel.

Firstly, Israel is regathered in the will of God. Secondly, she is sprinkled with clean water and cleansed from all filthiness and idolatry.

'Clean water' symbolizes the purifying action of God's Word (John 15:3; Ephesians 5:26). The Word of God is the *laver of cleansing* which sanctifies for the purifying of the flesh and spirit (Exodus 30:18; 2 Corinthians 7:1). When we receive the Word with meekness, it is able to save our souls – delivering us from all uncleanness and transforming us into the image of Jesus the Messiah.

The prophetic proclamation of the Word of God will play a significant role in the spiritual renewal of Israel. God will raise up apostles and prophets, as at the first, to declare His Word with signs and wonders by the power of the Holy Spirit!

> *'And the Word of God spread, and the number of the disciples multiplied greatly in Jerusalem, and a great many of the priests were obedient to the faith. And Stephen, full of faith and power, did great wonders and signs among the people.'*
> (Acts 6:7–8)

Thirdly, God promises to give His people a 'new heart' and to put a 'new spirit' within them. He declares that He will take away the hard, unresponsive heart with its propensity for unbelief and disobedience, and replace it with a 'heart of flesh' – a heart that is tender and responsive to His Spirit.

To a certain extent, this has begun to happen. Since the proclamation of Statehood in 1948, there has been a gradual but significant change in the general attitude of the Jewish people toward the Person of Jesus.

Three decisive turning points come to mind as one contemplates the changing spiritual climate of the nation. And in each case, natural things were shaken and removed, in order to make way for a new movement of God's Spirit and a further manifestation of God's Kingdom.

References

1. *Vine's Expository Dictionary of New Testament Words*, Riverside Book and Bible House, Iowa Falls, Iowa, p. 703.
2. *Alford's Greek Testament*, Baker Book, House, Grand Rapids, Michigan, Volume two, p. 936.

Chapter 6

A Time for War

*'To everything there is a season, a time for every purpose
under heaven ... a time of war, and a time of peace.'*
(Ecclesiastes 3:1, 8b)

Early Monday morning, June 5th, 1967. The Egyptian army
attacked in Sinai; by noon, Jordanian artillery was bombarding
New Jerusalem, and the Syrian army was shelling the *Kibbutzim* on the northern frontier.

In a lightning air strike, Israel destroyed four hundred Egyptian planes (nearly two-thirds of the enemy's combat air
strength) before they had left the ground.

Tuesday saw all eastern Jerusalem outside the ancient walls
in the hands of the Israelis, and contact made with the enclave
on Mount Scopus. On Wednesday came the historic breakthrough at St. Stephen's Gate, and suddenly the Temple area
was in Jewish hands.

By Thursday, the main Egyptian concentration had been put
out of action in the South, and Jewish forces were at the east
bank of the Suez Canal.

After an intense struggle in the Golan Heights, the Syrians
were finally dislodged from a complex network of fortifications
from where, for the past nineteen years, they had launched
repeated attacks on the defenceless *Kibbutzim* below. By Saturday, the road lay open to Damascus, forty miles away!

In less than a week Israel had enlarged her territory from
8,000 to 26,000 square miles. The flag of David now flew over

the east bank of the Suez Canal, the Gaza Strip, Sharm-El-Sheik on the Gulf of Aqaba, Judea and Samaria (the so-called 'West Bank' appropriated by Jordan in 1948), the Golan Heights, and most importantly, the Old City of Jerusalem.

This conflict, popularly known as *The Six Day War*, significantly influenced the spiritual disposition of the Jewish people.

For the first time in almost 1,900 years, ancient Jerusalem was in Jewish hands, thus fulfilling the words of Jesus in Luke 21:24; *'And Jerusalem will be trampled by Gentiles until the times of the Gentiles are fulfilled.'*

Scenes of unashamed emotion attended the arrival of Israeli soldiers at the Western Wall. The holiest site of Judaism, the last surviving link with the Temple, was open to Jews for the first time in nineteen years, and under actual Jewish control for the first time in nineteen-hundred years!

In the words of one reporter:

> 'Israeli soldiers were walking about the city as in a dream. Tears rolled down their faces. They did not bother to take cover from Arab snipers. They had realized the 2,000 year-old prophecy of recovering Jerusalem. When they saw the Wailing Wall, they broke out in a dead run until they fell to their knees at the Wall. There they sobbed, when victory should have made them exult. The mournful bleating of the shofar horn sounded. Unshaven, red-eyed soldiers, their combat uniforms stained with sweat and blood, donned their skullcaps, opened small leather-bound prayer books and rocked back and forth as they chanted, "Thank the Lord, for the Lord has been kind." Beyond the Wall, heavy firing still could be heard. But the war was forgotten.'[1]

Some 250,000 Jews streamed to the Western Wall for the Festival of *Shavuot* (Weeks or Pentecost) which fell that year on June 14th. In some mysterious way Israel had recovered her soul.

The discordant notes of the *shofar* that resounded from the Wall signalled both the restoration of a link with the past and the dawn of a new day of redemption.

Since that time, the Jewish people have displayed a new warmth and openness toward the Person of Jesus. For the first time in many centuries, they have begun to claim Him as one of their own.

During this same period many Christians have become aware of God's love for the Jewish people and His end-time purposes for the Jewish nation. The 'heart of stone' – the indifference, callousness and self-righteousness that has existed for centuries – is gradually being replaced by a 'heart of flesh'.

More and more Christians are becoming sensitive to God's concern for His ancient covenant people. New attitudes of love and acceptance, and new dimensions of understanding and responsibility are resulting in meaningful relationships between Jews and Christians.

The *Yom Kippur* War

The second major event to significantly influence the spiritual disposition of the Israeli population was the *Yom Kippur* war of October, 1973.

Yom Kippur (the Day of Atonement) is the most sacred day of the Jewish calendar year. Latin and Oriental Jews (the *Shephardim*) also call it 'The Day of Judgment'.

Historically, it was the day on which the High Priest would enter the Holy of Holies to make atonement or propitiation for the sins of the people (Leviticus 16).

During the ceremony two goats were presented before the Lord. One goat was slain and its blood was sprinkled by the High Priest before the Mercy Seat. Prayer was then offered over the other goat and the sins of the nations were transferred to it by the laying on of hands. The *scapegoat* was then led out of the temple and banished to the wilderness.

In modern times, Jews flock to the Synagogue to spend the day in prayer and total fasting. It is a day of repentance, in which the Jewish people pray for forgiveness and ask God to write and seal their names in the Book of the Living.

At 2 pm on October 6th, 1973, as many Israelis, including soldiers at the fronts, were observing the Day of Atonement with fasting and prayer, massive Egyptian and Syrian offensives began across the Suez Canal and in the Golan Heights.

Ranged along the 110 miles of the west bank of the Suez Canal was one of the largest standing armies in the world, comprising some 800,000 men, over 2,000 tanks, 150 anti-aircraft missile batteries, and 500 front-line planes.

Across the other side of the Suez Canal, along Israel's *Bar Lev Line*, some 500 army reservists, each outnumbered two hundred to one, valiantly resisted for five hours before capitulating to the Egyptian forces.

The Syrians launched their offensive with 1,400 tanks, and during the first three days recaptured much of the Golan Heights that had been lost in 1967, advancing almost to the edge of the plain of Galilee.

Egypt and Syria should have defeated Israel, but were inexplicably prevented from doing so. Having met and conquered the first lines of Israeli resistance and with the Land lying virtually open before them, the Egyptians and Syrians stopped.

Prime Minister Golda Meir described the gravity of those first few days:

> 'The shock wasn't only over the way in which the war had started, but also the fact that a number of our basic assumptions were proven wrong; the low probability of an attack in October, the certainty that we would get sufficient warning before any attack took place and the belief that we would be able to prevent the Egyptians from crossing the Suez Canal. The circumstances could not possibly have been worse. In the first two or three days of the war, only a thin line of brave young men stood between us and disaster. And no words of mine can ever express the indebtedness of the people of Israel to those boys on the Canal and on the Golan Heights. They fought, and fell, like lions, but at the start they had no chance.'[2]

The conflict was bitter and bloody, and for Israel the price of victory, in terms of human life, was enormous. Of the tens of thousands of Israelis summoned from homes and synagogues to answer the call to arms, 2,522 never returned.

God is the supreme Lord of history. The fact that God allowed Israel's enemies to attack her on *Yom Kippur*, 'The Day of Judgment', is itself a testimony to God's dealings with His people. God used Egypt and Syria in 1973 just as He used nations in Biblical times to judge the waywardness and backsliding of His people.

But one may ask, 'What sins occasioned the meting out of judgment on *Yom Kippur*, 1973?'

In order to properly answer that question, we must understand the nature of God and the principles of His Kingdom. The Psalmist cried, *'If You, LORD, should take note of iniquities, O LORD, who could stand? But there is forgiveness with You, that You may be feared'* (Psalm 130:3–4).

God is longsuffering and gracious, full of mercy and ready to forgive! However, there is one sin that God will not tolerate, even for a moment, and that is the sin of pride.

> *'God resists the proud ... these six things the LORD hates, yes, seven are an abomination to Him: a proud look...'*
> (James 4:6; Proverbs 6:16–17)

Furthermore, God says, *'I am the LORD, that is My Name; and My glory I will not give to another, nor My praise to graven images'* (Isaiah 42:8).

Following the remarkable military victories of 1948 and 1967, and the extraordinary achievements of the nation during her first twenty-five years of independence, certain strains of arrogance and self-sufficiency began to appear in the popular attitude. This was further compounded by the tough, independent spirit which characterized the early pioneers and continued, in the ensuing years, to undergird the nation's fight for survival.

The *Yom Kippur* War dramatically decimated the pride and self-assurance of the Jewish people. Shock and horror at the sight of permanently maimed soldiers returning from the battlefield, together with the names of many who would never return, plunged Israel into a crisis of introspection and recrimination.

Respected Bible teacher and author Lance Lambert, an eye-witness of the *Yom Kippur* War, described the attitudinal meta-morphosis that took place during and after the conflict:

'There are many signs of a very deep work taking place within the Israeli nation. Golda Meir said in a speech which I found one of the most moving I have ever heard, "There is no Jew in Israel can say that he is the same today as he was on the eve of *Yom Kippur*. I don't believe I will ever be the same." Bibles and prayer books were in demand above all else by the soldiers, and a controversy raged in the Hebrew Press as to whether the Field Rabbis (Service Chaplains) had failed in their duty or not ... there had been a run on Bibles during the first few weeks of the war, and there were none available ... For years no one except perhaps one lad here and there had ever asked for a Bible. Now suddenly thousands of men wanted them. One Israeli entertainer took a whole truckload of vodka, Bibles and prayer books to the Golan to distribute to the soldiers. It was very cold there, and he took the vodka to try and keep the boys warm. Surprisingly enough, however, it was not the vodka they wanted, but the Bibles...

'A recent report of interviews with soldiers has revealed that a surprisingly high number of them went into the war as atheists and came out as "believers". They are not believers as Christians understand the word, but believers in a Supreme Being. That is nevertheless a tremendous change of heart. One man told me, "I have never seen anything like it. The boys prayed before the battle, during battle and after battle. They spend time reading the Torah (the first five books of the Bible) and discussing it. I have never seen anything like it. Women normally pray, but not men." One great joy was the fact that the Israeli Cabinet officially sanctioned 15 minutes of Bible reading on the Israeli radio. This had never happened before but now the Bible is read for 15 minutes during peak listening time each evening.

'On November 5th, 1973, a few days before cease-fire,

the Chief Rabbi called Israel to prayer. That was the first
official Day of Prayer that the modern State of Israel had
ever had and virtually everyone responded to it. The synagogues were packed with people, there were never less
than 3,000 at the Western Wall in prayer and it was real
prayer from the heart. For those of us present on that
occasion it was unforgettable. For days afterward the sear-
ing tones of the Rabbi leading us in prayer burnt through
our soul. On few occasions can these ancient stones of the
Western Wall, spanning as they do the whole age from
Christ to the present time and crystalising the history,
sorrow, suffering and hopes of the Jewish people have ever
witnessed such prayer.'[3]

Displaying a unique understanding of God's nature and
appreciation of His ways, the prophet Isaiah declared, *'When
Your judgments are in the earth, the inhabitants of the world will
learn righteousness'* (Isaiah 26:9).

According to Mr Lambert's observation, the shaking of the
Yom Kippur War spawned a genuine humility, spiritual hunger
and prayerfulness in the lives of the Jewish people. Indeed,
such a response is in perfect unanimity with the purposes of
God both historically and prophetically.

Saddam, Scuds and Sealed Rooms

2.15 am, January 18th, 1991. The roar of air-raid sirens shat-
tered the stillness of the night in Israel's towns and cities,
warning of an impending Iraqi missile attack. From one end of
the country to the other people jumped out of bed and ran to
their 'sealed rooms'.

Once in their sealed rooms, people donned gas masks and
protective clothing, taped the doors and placed wet towels
dipped in a mixture of bleach and water along the aperture at
the bottom.

The scene could have been adapted from a science fiction
movie: four million Israelis sitting in hermetically sealed rooms
in the middle of the night, wearing gas masks – from the Prime
Minister to the army commander to the manual labourer!

After a quarter of an hour, the radio began broadcasting. Israel had been hit by Iraqi missiles, and civil defense teams with protective clothing had been sent out to determine whether or not they had been armed with chemical warheads. Medical teams were also on their way to the affected areas.

For about three hours that early Friday morning people sat with their gas masks on. After the first half hour, driblets of information began to come through Army Spokesman Nachman Shai. His voice was the Army's communication to a nation under siege, to each family, or worse yet, each individual, isolated in his room from the rest of the world.

Iraq, itself under attack from a multinational coalition led by the USA because of its brutal invasion and annexation of Kuwait, was responding by attacking Israel with Soviet made Scud missiles!

In that first attack, seven Scud missiles struck the Tel Aviv and Haifa areas. Seventeen people were slightly hurt, and many homes were damaged or destroyed.

Haga, Israel's Civil Defense, requested that no one leave his home the following day unless absolutely necessary. Businesses and schools were closed. Only vital industries asked that their employees report for work.

On Friday, January 18th, dawn broke on a nation paralysed by fear. In many ways, the scene resembled *Yom Kippur*, with hardly a car on the road. On *Yom Kippur*, however, there are always many pedestrians. On this day there were none. The nation was stunned and in shock.

The grocery stores were open, so people tentatively ventured out to buy some last minute things for the evening *Shabbat* meal and to stock up with extra supplies for the war. Everyone carried their gas masks with them!

A feeling of dread settled over the nation as the afternoon waned and people gathered around the *Shabbat* table. To compound the nervous strain, many people were unable to clearly hear the air-raid sirens in a closed house. The difficulty in distinguishing an actual alert from the mundane sounds of a car engine or an electric saw precipitated numerous 'false starts' and set many hearts pounding. People also woke up startled at the sound of thunder, thinking that a missile had landed nearby.

Finally, *Haga* announced that Israel must rouse herself and get back to work. For many Israelis, the simple act of leaving the house and going to work was a kind of forced therapy.

Saddam Hussein, the power hungry dictator of Iraq, had repeatedly threatened to incinerate half of Israel with deadly chemical weapons.

Styling himself on **Nebuchadnezzar**, the ancient King of Babylon who razed Jerusalem and carried the Jewish people off into captivity, and **Saladin**, the young Kurdish chief who defeated the Crusaders and restored Moslem rule to the Holy Land, Saddam received enthusiastic support from the local Arab population who saw him as a potential 'Saviour'.

To illustrate the point, residents of the disputed territories actually cheered from their rooftops and balconies as Iraqi missiles exploded in Tel Aviv!

Saddam's intentions were clear: to draw Israel into the war, and thereby shatter the fragile coalition arrayed against Iraq, a coalition that included such states as Egypt, Syria and Saudi Arabia.

Saddam believed that attacking Israel would make him a hero in the Arab world and would turn the conflict into another Arab-Israeli war. In such case, no Arab or Moslem state could oppose him!

The missile attacks created a perplexing dilemma for Israel. Traditional Israeli military doctrine called for an immediate and devastating response to any attack on the Jewish State. History attests to the fact that without such a policy, Israel would have long ceased to exist in the hostile neighbourhood of the Middle East.

The United States, however, exerted enormous pressure on Israel to stay out of the war and thus not endanger the stability of the coalition. In hindsight the ostensible threat to the coalition reads a little thin – it was most definitely in the interests of Saudi Arabia's self-preservation to remain in the coalition, regardless of Israel's involvement.

One also suspects that the State Department had an ulterior motive in asking Israel to let the United States do the fighting for them, a motive that surfaced months later in a speech by

President George Bush in which he claimed that American soldiers had risked their lives for Israel during the Gulf War, thereby implying an indebtedness on the part of the Jewish State which was utilized as a point of leverage in the ensuing peace negotiations.

The policy of restraint, however, won Israel praise from the USA and the international community. Israel, which is used to being everyone's favourite whipping boy, basked in the glory. The policy was also popular at home. Opinion polls showed that at least 70 percent of Israelis believed that the time was not right for retaliation.

But some Israelis were upset that the only time Israel gets any sympathy is when she is on the receiving end of harsh treatment. One former general said that the world is in love with the image of Israel as 'Samson the Weakling!'

Purim Joy

The bid to liberate Kuwait, codenamed *Operation Desert Storm*, ended at midnight February 27th, with the retreat and surrender of Iraqi occupational forces. The end of the Gulf War also meant, for the time being at least, the end of Iraqi missile attacks on Israel.

Most significantly, the war ended on the first day of *Purim*, the Feast that commemorates the deliverance of the Jews of Ancient Persia in the time of Queen Esther. Through God's miraculous intervention, the wicked ruler *Haman* was destroyed and his schemes of mass destruction were nullified.

Thousands of Israelis poured into the streets to celebrate *Purim*, many of them wearing traditional costumes and indulging in traditional revelries. But this celebration held special significance and contained a new dimension of spiritual reality.

The spirit of *Haman*, incarnated in the person of Saddam Hussein, had again been defeated and the Jewish people had again been preserved! Many people were quick to make a pun, because in Hebrew *Haman* rhymes with *Saddam*.

The comments of the late Rabbi Marc Tanenbaum, former

international relations director of the American Jewish Committee, make very interesting reading from the prophetic perspective:

> '...Purim symbolizes the Jewish confrontation with evil in every century and in practically every society in which Jews lived. Purim is thus a celebration of the Jewish will to survive and prevail. The moral assurance that Purim provides for prevailing over Hamans and their murderous designs against Jews is needed more in the year of Saddam Hussein than at any time since the Nazi Holocaust. The launching of Scud missiles into Israel's major population centres of Tel Aviv and Haifa is the first time such massive onslaughts against civilian areas has taken place since the founding of Israel.
>
> 'Hussein's sadistic rhetoric against Israel reads like an updated version of Haman's advice to King Ahasuerus (435–464 BCE): "If it please the king, let it be written that they be destroyed." Haman is long dead, but his pathological anti-Jewish hatred lives on in the brutal mind of Iraq's latest Nebuchadnezzar.'[4]

The joy and rejoicing notwithstanding, the cost to Israel in terms of property damage, losses to the tourism industry, losses in production and revenue due to work days missed during the state of emergency, and defense expenditure in maintaining a maximum state of alert and in supplying civil defense needs such as gas masks for the entire population, was enormous.

The finance ministry estimated that the war cost the Israeli economy no less than thirteen billion dollars! Actual property damage was estimated to be three billion dollars!

In 39 Scud missile strikes, miraculously only 13 people died (one directly from a Scud, and twelve from heart attacks and gas mask related accidents).

But the greatest cost of all was the psychological trauma experienced by ordinary men, women and children, who, through no fault of their own, suddenly found themselves catapulted to the front lines of the battlefield, albeit still in their lounge rooms! For this was Israel's first *civilian war*.

Israel's Philharmonic music director, **Zubin Mehta**, visited some of the missile damaged areas in Tel Aviv with Mayor Shlomo Lahat. 'The children in buildings near the blasts were so frightened that they wouldn't even come out of their shelters hours afterwards,' said Mehta. 'The mayor had to personally persuade them that it was safe for them to come out.'[5]

Psychologists said that most children were unable to understand what was causing them to be suddenly swept out of bed by their parents, placed in plastic bags or gas masks as sirens wailed, and then subjected to the terror of a loud explosion. The trauma was less intense for children in other parts of the country, but only marginally.

Elderly people, many of them living alone, were also very frightened, but it was the holocaust survivors who suffered the most. The prospect of sudden poisoning by gas was a realization of their most terrible nightmare and many found it almost too hard to bear.

A Jerusalem mother shared her feelings after watching over her five children while her husband served in civil defence during six threatened air raids: 'I was prepared for this war. But when it struck I found I wasn't really prepared at all. The attacks brought undiscovered fear. Yet I knew the Lord was with us.'

Another woman said, 'The gas masks are like death masks to the children. You cannot put them on peacefully. And it is even worse for the young babies put into the plastic boxes. Please pray the Lord will give grace at this time. That these children will not be scarred with traumatic memories.'[6]

A Western Jewish immigrant candidly described the disruption to family relationships and daily routines:

'Though, individually, we have as much chance of being hit by a Scud missile as we have of winning the lottery, the cloud of fear that hangs over our heads has broken our sleep patterns, changed our daily routines and created tension between husband and wife, parent and child. Casualties cannot be measured only in the numbers of wounded or killed, or property destroyed; they must be measured in terms of trauma to the national psyche ... On the night of the first alarms, my wife and I did a fairly reasonable job of rounding up five children, donning their masks and sealing the door. But my wife, an asthmatic, had difficulty breathing through the mask, a difficulty compounded by fumes from the chlorine-soaked towel at the bottom of our door. She began to hyperventilate – though neither of us realized it at the time – and panicked silently.

'When we were able to remove the masks, she began crying uncontrollably. In her mind, the children, who had been lying safely next to us with their masks on, were dying; their occasional coughing was a reaction to poison gases that had seeped into our room. I tried to comfort her, but to no avail. Then I turned my attention to the children, who were colouring in books purchased for the occasion. "Mommy's just happy that we're safe," I assured them. They weren't assured. My turn to fall apart came Saturday night. After three alarms the night before, and three days of being cooped up with the children, my temper was in rare bad form ... my routine had been thrown off and I was climbing the walls. I resent some of the disruptions to our lives. I have never attached any great significance to my beard, but I am uncomfortable with the idea that I was forced to shave it off; there is an unpleasant association with the Jews in Europe. I certainly resent the fears to which my children have been subjected. "I was scared," my daughter wrote on Saturday night, when she tried to recollect her feelings of the first attack. "I didn't want that gas bomb to fall. I felt that I was going to watch my brothers die. And it got me angry to see them taking off the masks with such carelessness."'[7]

World Jewish Congress vice president, **Isi Leibler**, described the mental and emotional stress of life in Israel during the Gulf War:

'... everybody feels the great weight of the unknown. It's not just the Scuds that generate this tension, although the damage these missiles have caused is frightening to behold. Thousands of homes have been damaged, many people are in a state of shock; just about everybody you speak to has had a close friend or relative who has been affected in one way or another. Nevertheless, it is miraculous that so far, despite the physical devastation, the casualties have been so minimal – less than a bad day on the roads ... the underlying tension comes, not from the missiles, but from the fear that the "Butcher of Baghdad" may yet do everything possible to fulfil his terrible promise and rain gas, chemicals and other weapons of mass destruction on the Jewish State. It is impossible to convey the feeling of living under this threat. The IDF spokesman Nachman Shai told me that every person sitting in a sealed room with a gas mask on has, so to speak, undergone "a second *brit mila* which he shares with the people of Israel". People's lives have changed ... In addition to the concern there is anger and frustration. This is Israel's first war in which civilians are on the front-line, while the IDF must gnash its teeth and stand idly by. They yearn to react ... no one has ever fought Israel's wars for it. We are living in an extraordinary period. Religious and secular all agree that a divine force or some other element of providence is watching over them...

'It would seem that there was something almost providential about Saddam's miscalculation with Kuwait and his subsequent refusal to even contemplate the face-saving formula that the French and others pleaded with him to accept, which would have enabled him to withdraw and retain power. It is almost a repeat of the biblical story, when Pharaoh's heart was hardened by God who encouraged him not to accept the compromises that were offered to him ... Another miracle. In the midst of missile attacks and threats of poison gas the Soviet *Olim* have continued to pour in, receiving their gas masks on arrival ... the shared experience that these Soviet migrants undergo with Israelis virtually on arrival, sitting out Saddam Hussein's

deadly missile attacks in sealed rooms, has greatly acceler-
ated their psychological integration into Israel, from a process that would have taken months or even years – to days
... The magnificent spirit of the people of Israel under
adversity has to be seen to be appreciated. Volunteers fight
over who can assist in providing services for new *olim*. If
only on a temporary basis, all the petty divisions are sus-
pended. Even Israel's notoriously ill-mannered taxi drivers
become polite and helpful. Prime Minister Yitzhak Shamir
is hailed by leftist Yossi Sarid as the "right leader in the
right place at the right time." [8]

Faith in the Trenches

'God is our refuge and strength,' declared the Psalmist, *'a very
present help in trouble. Therefore we will not fear...'* (Psalm
46:1, 2)

Trouble is a servant to bring us to faith in the God of salvation. This kind of faith, which comes to people when they are
under bombardment from Scud missiles, or sitting with their
children in gas-masks, has been called *faith in the God of the
trenches*.

Theologians and philosophers tend not to be impressed with
this sort of instant religion, but in the words of Australian
journalist **Sam Lipski**,

'...when you speak to residents of Ramat Gan, as I have
done this week, you understand why it is perfectly human to
be imperfectly religious when the windows of your flat have
just been blown out and the apartment building across the
road has been demolished. If at that point you are praying
with the deepest *kavanah* to the *Ribbono Shel Olam* to save
you and your children, even if you have never set foot inside
a shule, we should assume that He will understand, even if
the theologians and philosophers don't.' [9]

Indeed, there were many signs of a general 'turning to God'
during the Gulf crisis. An estimated 20,000 Orthodox Jews

massed at the Western Wall on the Monday prior to the first missile attack, reciting psalms and *slichot* prayers of repentance to prevent war.

Many of the worshippers were fasting. Tears flowed copiously as the cantor recited psalms traditionally said during times of tribulation. They ended with the *Avinu Malkeinu* prayer and blasts from dozens of shofars.

Dr Steven Lorch, principal of Mount Scopus College in Melbourne, Australia, was visiting Israel when she came under missile attack. He discovered that in such circumstances, routine synagogue services are transformed into dynamic encounters with spiritual reality:

'In this situation, in these times, even the familiar becomes new and distinctive. Old associations are supplanted by new understandings, and abstract ideas take on personal meaning and immediacy. To the untrained eye and ear, Friday evening services at the neighbourhood synagogue in Yemin Moshe last night were routine and unexceptional. No special prayers were offered, no particularly appropriate psalms were added. In fact, with the previous emergency having ended less than 12 hours before, and with the expectation of further missile attacks at any time (the first of these emergencies that night took place three hours later), prayers were recited rapidly and, on the surface, at least, perfunctorily.

'But I sensed a particularly charged atmosphere in the synagogue, one in which mothers fearful for their children, fathers who had received word that they were to be called up into reserve duty the following week, and children still adjusting to a reality of gas masks and confinement found new poignancy in the words they were reciting. Each person in synagogue, I daresay, discovered resonance in different prayers and phrases, each in accordance with his or her own spirit of the moment. As for me, the following passage from the *b'racha* preceding the *Amidah*, jumped out of the page of the siddur at me:

'"Lay us down to sleep, O Lord our God, in peace, and

make us rise, our King, in life ... Protect our going out
and our coming in, in life and in peace for now and
forever, and spread over us Your canopy of peace.
Blessed are You, O God, Who spreads the canopy of
peace upon us, upon His entire people, the house of
Israel, and upon Jerusalem." '10

Following the first wave of Scud missile attacks on Haifa and
Tel Aviv and the warnings in Jerusalem, *Ma'ariv*, one of the
largest Hebrew newspapers, printed the full text of Jeremiah
chapters 50 and 51 (in which God decrees the destruction of
Babylon) under the title, 'Take a Tip from the Prophets'.

As Israel survived each onslaught, the talk in military and
political circles was not of luck, but of 'miracles'. Secular
Israelis displayed a new willingness to talk about God and Bible
prophecy. For Jews in the Diaspora, the war brought a fresh
awareness of their spiritual and cultural heritage, and forged
greater links with the Land of Israel.

Even as the heat of the sun causes fruit to ripen and flowers to
bloom in the natural realm, so the pressure of circumstances
during the Gulf crisis produced a spiritual change in the hearts
and lives of the Jewish people – a turning to God and an
opening up to spiritual realities. In this sense, Israel's Gulf War
experience foreshadowed the restoration spoken of by the
prophet Zechariah.

Standing in the Gap

As always, God was one step ahead of Satan in the Gulf War,
and had His people strategically placed to 'head the enemy off
at the pass'. A prophetic prayer conference, planned some
twelve months in advance, commenced in Jerusalem on January
15th, the very day set down by the Allies as the deadline for
Iraq to leave Kuwait!

God providentially brought 120 believers from the nations to
Jerusalem as the Gulf War broke out to stand in the gap for the
protection of Israel and help prepare the way spiritually for His
end time purposes to be manifested in the Middle East.

The intercessors testified to the grace of Divine Appointment – the ability to be in the right place at the right time to turn what the enemy meant for evil into eternal good:

> 'We are experiencing the most significant time of prayer that we have ever had in any previous conference. God, in His absolute sovereignty and foreknowledge had timed this week to fall in perfect line with the most dramatic changes in the history of our world since World War II. An unusually strong spirit of prophecy and of prayer has taken hold of us, and we are extremely encouraged by the fact that from all corners of the world many are standing together with us for the fulfilment of God's eternal purposes with Israel and the Middle East.'[11]

God not only used the Gulf War to awaken Israel to her Divine destiny, but also to alert the Church to its imperative responsibility.

The experience of these 120 intercessors is a prophetic shape of things to come in the final epoch of human history. More than all the sermons in the world, this sovereign act of God defined the nature of the Church's principal ministry to Israel – that of upholding her before the Throne of Grace and praying into effect the purpose of God.

Called into Covenant

Like the rudder on a great ship, God is gradually turning the hearts of the Jewish people back to Himself. He is in the process of giving them a new heart and of placing His Spirit within them.

The signs of this are everywhere. There is an unmistakable trend back to religion. Non-religious *kibbutzim* have had to build synagogues to keep their young people. State schools were obliged to include three to five classes on the Bible weekly so that the pupils would not change to religious schools. In 1955, 42% of the Israeli population called themselves atheists; in 1988, the figure had fallen to just 10%.

Most important of all, Jews in increasing numbers are coming to recognize and accept Jesus as Messiah. Whereas it was once hard to find even one Jewish believer in towns and villages in Israel, one can now find groups of Messianic Jews throughout the country. Reports are regularly coming to hand of supernatural visitations and revelations of the Lord Jesus to spiritually hungry Israelis.

The number of believers at this stage is small compared with the ingathering that will surely take place. However, the sluice gate is open and water has started to flow. What is now a trickle will become a river, and the river will become a torrent that cannot be stopped.

God's dealings with Israel will issue in a new and eternal relationship between the Lord and His Ancient People. He says, *'I will be your God and you shall be My people.'*

The prophet Jeremiah sheds further light on the ultimate goal and end result of God's dealings with Israel:

> *'"Behold, the days are coming," says the LORD, "When I will make a new covenant with the house of Israel and with the house of Judah – Not according to the covenant that I made with their fathers in the day that I took them by the hand to bring them out of the land of Egypt, My covenant which they broke, though I was a Husband to them," says the LORD.*
>
> *'"But this is the covenant that I will make with the house of Israel after those days," says the LORD: "I will put My law in their minds, and write it on their hearts; and I will be their God, and they shall be My people. No more shall every man teach his neighbour, and every man his brother, saying, 'Know the LORD,' for they all shall know Me, from the least of them to the greatest of them," says the LORD. "For I will forgive their iniquity, and their sin I will remember no more."'* (Jeremiah 31:31–34)

Israel's inability to keep the Mosaic Covenant occasioned the establishment of a new and better covenant based on better promises. Faithfulness and obedience, the missing ingredients of the Mosaic Covenant, are implicit in the New. Central to this dynamic change in Israel's behaviour is the 'Divine surgery' God performs on the hearts and minds of His people.

God describes the heart of man as *'deceitful above all things and desperately wicked or incurably sick'* (Jeremiah 17:9). For this reason, Jesus declared that *'unless one is born again, he cannot see the Kingdom of God'* (John 3:3). The 'New Birth' involves both a change of heart and a change of mind.

When one believes on Messiah Jesus he is born again, not of corruptible seed but incorruptible, through the Word of God which lives and abides forever (1 Peter 1:23). The same Holy Spirit that hovered over the virgin Mary and caused her to conceive Messiah, hovers over truly repentant men and women and makes them into new creatures in Messiah Jesus, created in the image of God in righteousness and true holiness (Ephesians 4:24).

This is precisely what will happen to the Jewish people as God pours on them the Spirit of Grace and Supplication and they look on Him whom they have pierced. Jeremiah describes the tremendous transformation that will take place in their innermost being:

> *'Then I will give them one heart and one way, that they may fear Me forever, for the good of them and their children after them. And I will make an everlasting covenant with them, that I will not turn away from doing them good; but I will put My fear in their hearts so that they will not depart from Me.'* (Jeremiah 32:39, 40)

The Jewish people will be initiated through faith into the New and Everlasting Covenant established by God in the Blood of His only begotten Son. In sharp contrast to former times, this relationship will be one of enduring intimacy. *'They shall all know Me,'* says the Lord, *'from the least of them to the greatest of them.'*

The knowledge of God will not be taught by rote or ceremony, but will be imparted through a personal relationship of living faith. There will be no more consciousness of sin among those who turn to the Lord, for the Blood of Messiah, Who through the Eternal Spirit offered Himself without spot to God, will purge their conscience from dead works to serve the Living God! Hallelujah!

References

1. *God's Timetable for the End of Time*, by Oral Roberts. Heliotrope Publications, Tulsa, Oklahoma, p. 24.
2. *My Life* by Golda Meir. Futura Publications, London, p. 360.
3. *Battle For Israel* by Lance Lambert, © 1975 Tyndale House Publishers, and used by permission of Kingsway Publications Ltd, 1 St. Anne's Road, Eastbourne, BN21 3UN, England.
4. *Australian Jewish News*, Melbourne Edition, February 29th, 1991.
5. *Israel News Digest*, by David Dolan. Published by Christian Friends of Israel, PO Box 1813, Jerusalem, 91015, Israel.
6. *Prayer for Israel* (NZ) Newsletter, by Murray Dixon. PO Box 1032, Palmerston North, New Zealand.
7. Excerpted from *For Us Casualties, Sweet Victory* by Joel Rebibo. The Jerusalem Post International Edition, February, 1991.
8. *Australian Jewish News*, Melbourne Edition, February 15th, 1991.
9. *Australian Jewish News*, Melbourne Edition, February 15th, 1991.
10. *Australian Jewish News*, Melbourne Edition, February 1st, 1991.
11. *Prayer for Israel* (NZ) Newsletter, by Murray Dixon. PO Box 1032, Palmerston North, New Zealand.

Chapter 7

God's Glory is the Key

'Therefore, whether you eat or drink, or whatever you do, do all to the glory of God.' (1 Corinthians 10:31)

In the words of the Westminster Catechism, 'The chief end of man is to enjoy God and glorify Him forever.' Such a statement of purpose contrasts sharply with the humanistic philosophy of this world which places man at the centre of the universe.

The truth is that God alone is the source of life; He is also the centre around which the universe revolves and by which it is sustained; furthermore, He is the supreme goal of creation.

The Apostle Paul expressed the Biblical worldview in his epistle to the Christians at Rome:

'For of Him and through Him and to Him are all things, to Whom be glory forever. Amen.' (Romans 11:36)

Creation exists for the glory of its Creator. Man is the crown jewel of creation, and as such, possesses a unique capacity to glorify and honour his Maker.

As Christians, we need to recover a 'God-centred' theology; otherwise, we will never understand God's dealings with the Church, the nations, and Israel.

Election and Grace

One of the arguments most frequently raised to refute Israel's place in God's purpose is the unworthiness of the Jews. A

107

misguided notion, which unfortunately is foundational to some longstanding theological concepts and religious attitudes, states that 'after what the Jews did to Jesus, they do not deserve God's mercy or blessing – they are fit for nothing more than hell and judgment.'

However, Israel's place in God's purpose is based entirely on the sovereign choice and unmerited favour of God. The New Testament uses two words to describe the legal basis of Israel's position in God's economy: one is **election** and the other is **grace**.

Election speaks of God's right to choose and use whoever He wants to, in order to fulfil His purpose. The word 'election' also contains the idea of 'conscription' and 'apprehension'. It does not exclude the necessity of willingness and obedience on the part of the one who is called, however, the emphasis is on the power of God's choice. He whom God chooses, He also compels!

Grace speaks of the undeserved kindness of God toward entirely unworthy objects. God extends favour to those who could never earn it. He honours their desire to please Him and accepts their faith as righteousness. God loves simply because of Who He is. His nature compels Him to show mercy on those who do not merit it.

As Christians, our place in God's Kingdom is also based entirely on His **election** and **grace**. We do not deserve God's grace and blessing any more than the Jews. In fact, in the 2,000 years of her history, the Church has been scarcely more obedient to God than was Israel in the previous 2,000 years! Jew and Gentile alike stand in absolute need of God's unfathomable kindness.

For this reason, Christians ought not to feel superior in any way to God's Ancient Covenant People. Wilful ignorance or negligence of Israel's place in God's purpose opens the door to spiritual pride and deception.

Christians have nothing whatsoever in which to boast, except the Cross of the Lord Jesus. Our attitude, therefore, should be one of 'fear' – humble gratitude and reverential awe. When we truly see our utter dependence on God's election and grace, we will have no trouble accepting the Jewish people on the same basis.

The Apostle Paul clearly defined the proper attitude of Christians toward the Jewish people in the light of God's election and grace:

> *'And if some of the branches were broken off, and you, being a wild olive tree, were grafted in among them, and with them became a partaker of the root and fatness of the olive tree, Do not boast against the branches. But if you boast, remember that you do not support the root, but the root supports you. You will say then, "Branches were broken off that I might be grafted in." Well said. Because of unbelief they were broken off, and you stand by faith. Do not be haughty, but fear. For if God did not spare the natural branches, He may not spare you either.*
>
> *Therefore consider the goodness and severity of God: on those who fell, severity; but toward you, goodness, if you continue in His goodness. Otherwise you also will be cut off. And they also, if they do not continue in unbelief, will be grafted in, for God is able to graft them in again ... For I do not desire, brethren, that you should be ignorant of this mystery, lest you should be wise in your own opinion...'*
>
> (Romans 11:17–23, 25)

Israel's role in God's eternal purpose is a mystery that can only be understood through revelation. However, God does not desire us to be ignorant of this truth. On the contrary, the blindness of the Church in regard to the restoration of Israel is a continual grief to the Father's heart.

God's New Thing

In Isaiah chapter 43 there is a key of knowledge that unlocks the mystery of Israel's regathering and restoration. In graphic terms God describes the suffering of the Jewish Diaspora throughout the centuries, and in particular, the suffering of European Jewry in the holocaust of World War Two:

> *'When you pass through the waters, I will be with you; and through the rivers, they shall not overflow you. When you walk through the fire, you shall not be burned, nor shall the flame scorch you.'*

Moreover, the Lord declares that He will gather a remnant from the North, South, East and West and will bring them to Zion. God Himself will make a way for them to return. He will deal with the obstacles. He will conquer all resistance. He will open up 'the Red Sea' once again.

The magnificence and greatness of this regathering will surpass even that of the Exodus from Egypt, some 4,000 years ago!

Highlighting the uniqueness of this end-time regathering, God says, *'Do not remember former things, nor consider things of old. Behold, I will do a new thing, now it shall spring forth, shall you not know it? I will even make a road in the wilderness...'*

This century we have witnessed the fulfilment of the Word of God in a remarkable way. A people have been regathered, a nation has been reborn – God has done a 'new thing' in the earth!

And in this midst of this prophecy God reveals the purpose of Israel's existence and the secret of her destiny:

> *'... bring my sons from afar, and My daughters from the ends of the earth – everyone who is called by My Name, whom I have created for My glory; I have formed him, yes, I have made him. This people I have formed for Myself; they shall declare My praise.'*   (Isaiah 43:6–7, 21)

God has formed Israel for Himself; her reason for being is to glorify God. The end result of God's dealings with Israel is that she will declare His praise!

One of the major themes of the Bible is the glory of God. The express purpose of Jesus' life was to honour and obey His Heavenly Father. At the conclusion of His earthly ministry He declared: *'I have glorified You on the earth. I have finished the work You have given Me to do'* (John 17:4).

Likewise, the goal of the Church is to glorify God in the earth – to disseminate His knowledge among the nations through prophetic proclamation and practical demonstration of His Word.

The glory and honour of God should be the focus of every Christian's heart and life – the chief motivation and ultimate objective of all he says and does (1 Corinthians 10:31). The crowning reward of our service is that men will see our good works and glorify our Father in heaven (Matthew 5:16).

The Heavenly Father takes supreme delight in the glory of His Son. He is directing history to one end – that Messiah should be all and in all. The universe is destined to be consummated under the Headship of Jesus the Messiah (Ephesians 1:10). Every knee will bow to His Majesty and every tongue will acknowledge His Lordship, to the glory of God the Father (Philippians 2:11).

The Church is Messiah's Body and is therefore His primary avenue of revelation to the world. This does not mean, however, that the Church is the only instrument through which God accomplishes His purposes.

For example, God has built into natural creation a revelation of His Divine Nature and redemptive purpose: *'The heavens declare the glory of God...'* (Psalm 19:1 and Romans 1:20). God continues to speak through the elements of nature, warning and if necessary judging men, in the hope that they will repent of their sins and obey the truth.

Furthermore, God uses ungodly rulers, the 'Nebuchadnezzars' of this world, to fulfil His purposes. To Pharaoh God said, *'Even for this same purpose I have raised you up, that I might show My power in you, and that My Name might be declared in all the earth'* (Romans 9:17). God even causes the wrath of man to praise Him!

Is it any wonder then, that God has chosen to use Israel for His glory and His end-time purposes? God is using and will continue to use Israel, in spite of her unbelief and disobedience, to fulfil His prophetic Word and to magnify His Name among the nations.

They Shall Know That I Am the Lord

The prophet Ezekiel sheds further light on Israel's role in God's end-time plan. Once again, there is a key of knowledge hidden in the prophecy, which, when discovered, unlocks the mystery of God's dealings with Israel and the nations.

The key is a simple phrase that appears over sixty times: *'Then they shall know that I am the LORD.'* The ultimate goal of God's dealings with men and nations is that they might know that He is the Lord – the Omnipotent Creator and Sovereign Ruler of all things. Israel has a unique part to play in the revelation and dissemination of the knowledge of God in the last days.

In chapter 36, God declares that He will gather the exiles out of all the nations where He has dispersed them and will settle them once again in their own land. Twenty-one times God says, *'I will.'*

> *'I will turn to you ...'*
> *'I will multiply ...'*
> *'I will cause ...'*
> *'I will sanctify ...'*
> *'I will not let ...'*
> *'I will take ...'*
> *'I will give ...'*
> *'I will sprinkle ...'*
> *'I will put ...'*
> *'I will deliver ...'*
> *'I will increase ...'*

Clearly, the will of God is the primary factor in Israel's rebirth and development. This fact alone should be a deterrent to Israel's enemies. To oppose the principle of Israel's existence is to resist the will of Almighty God. And in a contest like that, I know whose side I would rather be on!

It does not require much faith to understand why God uprooted the Jewish people from the Land and scattered them among the nations.

God Himself says,

> '... *when the house of Israel dwelt in their own land, they defiled it by their own ways and deeds; to Me their way was like the uncleanness of a woman in her customary impurity. Therefore I poured out My fury on them for the blood they had shed on the Land, and for their idols with which they had defiled it ... I judged them according to their ways and their deeds.'* (Ezekiel 36:17–19)

However, when it comes to understanding the rebirth of Israel, one must have a revelation of the motivation of God's heart. God is not regathering the Jews primarily for their own sake or because they deserve it.

Israel has been restored and continues to exist principally for the glory of God. Her rebirth as a nation in the closing days of human history is a masterstroke of Divine Genius, as God seeks to bring all nations into a fresh awareness of His power and glory.

It is important to understand that God does not bless us primarily for our own sake. The Church needs to be delivered from a 'consumer mentality'. God delights to bless us and to meet our needs so that through us He may be glorified in the earth!

All things are ours and all things are for our sake; but we exist for the sake of Messiah Jesus, and Messiah lives for the glory of the Father (1 Corinthians 3:21–23).

The motivation of God's heart in the regathering of the Jewish people is clearly expressed in the prophecy of Ezekiel:

> 'But I had concern for My holy Name, which the house of Israel had profaned among the nations wherever they went. Therefore say to the house of Israel, "Thus says the LORD God: 'I do not do this for your sake, O house of Israel, but for My holy Name's sake, which you have profaned among the nations wherever you went. And I will sanctify My great Name, which has been profaned among the nations, which you have profaned in their midst; and the nations shall know that I am the LORD,' says the LORD God, 'When I am hallowed in you before their eyes.'"'* (Ezekiel 36:21–23)

A sequence of prophetic events unfolds in the succeeding chapters of Ezekiel: The resurrection of the Jewish nation and the transformation thereof into an exceedingly great army ... A massive invasion by the combined forces of a Communist-Islamic alliance ... The miraculous annihilation of this evil confederacy through the sovereign intervention of God ... The reconciliation of Israel to the Lord and His manifest Presence in her midst!

Through each of these momentous phases, Israel is depicted as an instrument in the hand of the Lord, a vehicle through which He will be glorified in the eyes of the nations:

> '*I will set My sanctuary in their midst forevermore. My tabernacle also shall be with them; indeed I will be their God, and they shall be My people. The nations also will know that I, the LORD, sanctify Israel, when My sanctuary is in their midst forevermore.*' (Ezekiel 37:26–28)

> '*You will come up against My people Israel like a cloud, to cover the land. It will be in the latter days that I will bring you against My land, so that the nations may know Me, when I am hallowed in you, O Gog, before their eyes ... And I will bring him to judgment with pestilence and bloodshed; I will rain down on him, on his troops, and on the many peoples who are with him, flooding rain, great hailstones, fire and brimstone. Thus I will magnify Myself and sanctify Myself, and I will be known in the eyes of many nations. Then they shall know that I am the LORD.*' (Ezekiel 38:16, 22–23)

> '*And I will send fire on Magog and on those who live in security in the coastlands. Then they shall know that I am the LORD. So I will make My holy Name known in the midst of My people Israel, and I will not let them profane My holy Name anymore. Then the nations shall know that I am the LORD, the Holy One in Israel...*
>
> '*I will set My glory among the nations; all the nations shall see My judgment which I have executed, and My hand which I have laid on them. So the house of Israel shall know that I am the LORD their God from that day forward...*

> '... *Now I will bring back the captives of Jacob, and have mercy on the whole house of Israel; and I will be jealous for My holy Name* ... *when I have brought them back from the peoples and gathered them out of their enemies' lands, and I am hallowed in them in the sight of many nations*...'
>
> (Ezekiel 39:6–7, 21–22, 25, 27)

Living for the Glory of God

The prayer that Jesus taught His disciples to pray is both a model for praying and a pattern for living. In it the priorities of the Kingdom of Heaven are carefully unfolded, line upon line and precept upon precept.

The first priority in the life of a disciple is the knowledge of God – intimate relationship with *'Our Father'*. Secondly, there is a recognition and acknowledgment of His sovereign ruler-ship: *'Who art in Heaven'*.

Thirdly, there is the priority of the honour and glory of God: *'Hallowed by Thy Name'* And as God is duly honoured and glorified, *'His Kingdom comes and His will is done on earth as it is in Heaven'*.

Thus, the supreme motivation and goal of a disciple is to glorify God. And to this very end the nation of Israel has been manifested in the last of the last days. Can we do anything less than rejoice in that which God has created for the glory of His Name?

Chapter 8

A Banner for the Peoples

'Thus says the LORD *God: "Behold, I will lift My hand in
an oath to the nations, and set up My standard* (banner) *for
the peoples; they shall bring your sons in their arms; and
your daughters shall be carried on their shoulders."'*

(Isaiah 49:22)

The Hebrew word *'nec'*, translated 'ensign', 'standard' or 'banner', primarily denotes a standard as a rallying point or a flag as
a signal. It is derived from the primary root *'nacac'* which means
'to gleam from afar', that is, 'to be conspicuous'.

The Lord declares through the prophet Isaiah that the
regathering of the Jewish people and the rebirth of Israel is a
banner for the nations.

This may be interpreted three ways, each of which is correct
and essential for a complete understanding of God's prophetic
purpose.

Firstly, the rebirth of Israel as a nation among nations is a
banner to the Jewish Diaspora throughout the world. It is a
signal from the Lord that it is time for the Jewish people to
return home. It is a new day; the time of Zion's favour has
come. The Lord is building up Zion and will soon appear in
glory!

Hundreds of thousands of Jews from all over the world have
recognized and responded to the signal, rallying to the standard
of the Lord in *Eretz* Israel. Many more are yet to come, albeit
reluctantly.

Secondly, the rebirth of Israel is a banner of the Lord, uniquely designed to capture the attention of Gentile nations and governments. One only has to read the newspapers to realize just how successful Israel is in capturing the attention of the whole world!

This little nation of five million people, occupying less than one percent of the earth's surface, frequently dominates the news headlines. Whether she likes it or not, Israel is a banner raised up of God!

Thirdly, the rebirth of Israel is a signal or message from the Lord to the nations. Through Israel, God is declaring:

A. I am a God Who keeps covenant. Though men may fail and forsake Me, My faithfulness endures throughout all generations.
B. My Prophetic Word is absolutely true and can be totally relied on to come to pass. Heaven and earth may pass away, but My Word will never pass away.
C. The return of Jesus and the end of the age is at hand. Watch and pray that you do not fall into temptation or deception. Be prepared to stand before the judgment seat of Messiah.

Regathered, Regathered

The prophet Isaiah elaborates on the regathering of the exiles in chapter eleven:

> '*It shall come to pass in that day that the LORD shall set His hand again the second time to recover the remnant of His people who are left, from Assyria and Egypt, from Pathros and Cush, from Elam and Shinar, from Hamath and the islands of the sea. He will set up a banner for the nations, and will assemble the outcasts of Israel, and gather together the dispersed of Judah, from the four corners of the earth.*
>
> *Also the envy of Ephraim shall depart, and the adversaries of Judah shall be cut off; Ephraim shall not envy Judah, and Judah shall not harass Ephraim. But they shall fly down upon the shoulder of the Philistines toward the*

West; together they shall plunder the people of the East; they shall lay their hand on Edom and Moab; and the people of Ammon shall obey them.' (Isaiah 11:11–14)

Once again, the prophet declares that the end-time regathering of the Jewish people in their own Land will be a banner to the nations – a clear and unmistakable sign from the Living God.

Isaiah delivered this prophecy in the latter part of the Eighth Century BC, over one hundred years before Nebuchadnezzar conquered and destroyed Jerusalem in 586 BC. He prophesied that the Jewish people would be scattered and then regathered to their Land, not once but twice! He looked beyond the Babylonian captivity and the return to Jerusalem, and foresaw a second scattering and a second regathering.

The scope and magnitude of the regathering here described far exceeds that of the regathering that took place under the leadership of Zerubbabel, Ezra, and Nehemiah. The prophet listed the places from which the second regathering would take place: *Assyria* (Iraq), *Egypt*, *Cush* (Ethiopia), *Elam* (Iran), *Babylonia* (Iraq), *Hamath* (Syria), and the *islands* or *coastlands of the sea* – that is, all the other areas of the earth that border on the ocean.

Furthermore, Isaiah declared that the dispersed of Judah would be gathered from *the four corners of the earth* – that is, from all over the world. The rebirth of Israel in 1948 and the subsequent mass immigration of Jews from over seventy countries constitutes the only truly 'worldwide' regathering of Jewish exiles in history.

Israel has been regathered as one people, a united nation, exactly as Isaiah prophesied. The division and dissension that previously existed between the Northern and Southern Kingdoms, *Ephraim and Judah*, has been erased and forgotten.

The Prophetic Word then goes on to nominate two strategic geographical areas over which the reborn State of Israel will exercise control: *the shoulder of the Philistines*, and *Edom and Moab*.

'The Shoulder of the Philistines' refers to the coastal plain of

Canaan, known in modern times as **the Gaza Strip**. The ancient Philistines migrated to the coast of Canaan from Caphtor (Crete or islands to the north of it in the Aegean Sea) in the twelfth or thirteenth century BC.

The contemporary words *Palestine* and *Palestinian* are derived from the Biblical words *Philistia* and *Philistine*. However, it is important to note that *Philistia* only ever referred to the coastal strip in the South-Eastern littoral of the Mediterranean. The Jewish historian, Josephus, used the term *Palaistine* in the same restricted geographical sense.

After the Bar Kochbah rebellion of AD 132–135 the Romans changed the name of the Land to **Syria-Palestina** in an attempt to totally expunge the Jewish connection with *Eretz* Israel. Jerusalem became **Aelia Capitolina** and was rendered inaccessible to Jews for the next two hundred years!

The term *Palestine* was used by the Greek historian, Herodotus, in Fifth Century literature, to denote the entire Land of Israel. To my mind, it is yet another example of humanism's attempt to undermine Divine order by replacing that which is ordained of God with a counterfeit production of man.

Even modern Bible atlases publish maps of 'Palestine in the time of Christ.' The map may be right, but the title certainly isn't. The Land in the time of Christ – that is, the part of the Land in which Jesus lived and spent most of His time ministering, was called **Judea**, **Samaria**, and **Galilee**, not Palestine! (see Luke 3:1).

Israel is the Divine designation of the Promised Land. The name **Israel**, meaning 'Prince with God' or 'God-ruled,' is a mark of Divine ownership, a stamp of Divine sovereignty, and is therefore an expression of God's Kingdom on earth. Conversely, 'Palestine' is an expression of the spirit of antichrist that seeks to overthrow the rule of God.

'Edom, Moab and Ammon' are all found within the boundaries of modern day Jordan. The history of Jordan dates back to 1921, when Winston Churchill, British Secretary of the Colonies, partitioned 'Palestine' with a stroke of his pen, thus creating the mandatory territory of Trans-Jordan.

Churchill hoped that by presenting the Arabs with four-fifths of the total territory of 'Palestine,' he would placate their vociferous demands and smouldering anger.

American President Woodrow Wilson, a Christian and a student of the Scriptures, pressured his victorious World War One colleagues, the imperialist politicians, to behave morally and idealistically, and to observe the principle of 'the right of self-determination for all nations.' To this end, He protested against Churchill's and Britain's arbitrary partitioning of 'Palestine':

> 'The Zionist cause is tied to the security of Biblical boundaries and has in view the economic development of the country. This means that in the north Palestine should reach to the River Litani and the source of the streams of Mount Hermon; in the east it should include the Plains of Jaulon and Haran. Otherwise we would have a case of mutilation. I would like to remind you that neither Washington nor Paris have manifested opposition to the Zionist plan nor to securing indispensable Biblical boundaries...'[1]

Man proposes, but God disposes. Each war that has been thrust upon Israel has only served to enlarge her dominion. Little by little she is possessing the Land, and in the fulness of time she will occupy all the area allotted to her in the Covenant and purpose of God!

The Valley of Decision

The Bible teaches that the nations will be judged on the basis of their response to the 'Banner of the Lord' – the rebirth and regathering of Israel.

When God speaks a word or raises a banner, the nations cannot ignore it. There is only one choice: to obey or disobey the Truth; to accept or reject God's Message.

God has set Jerusalem and Israel 'in the midst of the nations' (Ezekiel 5:5) as a test case, to see if the nations will honour His sovereignty and obey His Word. The regathering of the Jewish people is a sovereign act of God and a fulfilment of His Prophetic Word. The attitude of the nations toward Israel therefore, is an accurate reflection of their attitude toward the Lord and His Word.

The prophet Joel portrays Israel as a 'watershed' in the international community, a 'plumbline' in the hand of the Lord with which He measures and judges the nations:

> *'For behold, in those days and at that time, when I bring back the captives of Judah and Jerusalem, I will also gather all nations, and bring them down to the valley of Jehoshaphat; and I will enter into judgment with them there on account of My people, My heritage Israel, whom they have scattered among the nations; they have also divided up My land ... Indeed, what have you to do with Me, O Tyre and Sidon, and all the coasts of Philistia? Will you retaliate against Me? But if you retaliate against Me, swiftly and speedily I will return your retaliation upon your own head...*
>
> *'Let the nations be wakened, and come up to the valley of Jehoshaphat; for there I will sit to judge all the surrounding nations. Put in the sickle, for the harvest is ripe. Come, go down; for the winepress is full, the vats overflow – for their wickedness is great. Multitudes, multitudes in the valley of decision! For the Day of the* LORD *is near in the valley of decision.'*   (Joel 3:1–2, 4, 12–14)

The name 'Jehoshaphat' literally means, 'Yahweh judges'. The Valley of Jehoshaphat, therefore, represents a place of judgment, and hence, is also called, **The Valley of Decision**.

The Judge is none other than Almighty God. The recipients of judgment are the nations, and the issue over which they are being judged is their treatment of Israel.

The judgment takes place in the time of Israel's restoration – *When I bring back the captives of Judah and Jerusalem*. Moreover, God closely identifies Himself with Israel at this time, calling them *My people*, *My heritage*, and their territory, *My Land*. In other words, God is saying, 'Inasmuch as you have done it unto Israel, you have done it unto Me!'

God is especially angry with the nations for removing the

Jewish people from the Land and dispersing them among the Gentiles, and for appropriating the Land for their own purposes! The word 'divide' means 'to partition' – something that the world has been trying to do with *Eretz* Israel since 1921!

It is important to note that the decision, in this case, is the Lord's. Judgment belongs unto God.

Sheep and Goats

The Lord Jesus described the end-time judgment of nations in the parable of the Sheep and the Goats, recorded in Matthew chapter twenty-five:

> 'When the Son of Man comes in His glory, and all the holy angels with Him, then He will sit on the throne of His glory. And all the nations will be gathered before Him, and He will separate them one from another, as a shepherd divides his sheep from the goats...
>
> Then the King will say to those on His right hand, "Come, you blessed of My Father, inherit the Kingdom prepared for you from the foundation of the world: For I was hungry and you gave Me food; I was thirsty and you gave me drink; I was a stranger and you took me in; I was naked and you clothed Me; I was sick and you visited Me; I was in prison and you came to Me ... Inasmuch as you did it to one of the least of these My brethren, you did it to Me."
>
> Then He will also say to those on the left hand, "Depart from Me, you cursed, into the everlasting fire prepared for the devil and his angels: For I was hungry and you gave Me no food; I was thirsty and you gave Me no drink; I was a stranger and you did not take Me in, naked and you did not clothe Me, sick and in prison and you did not visit Me ... Inasmuch as you did not do it to one of the least of these, you did not do it to Me."' (Matthew 25:31–46)

Jesus could not have made it any clearer: The scene is the Last Judgment, and all nations are gathered before the Throne of the Lamb. Each nation is judged according to its works. At stake is a place in Messiah's eternal Kingdom.

As in the Book of Joel, the primary issue of judgment is how the nations have treated Jesus' brethren. For whatever the nations do to Jesus' brethren, they do to Him, and are judged accordingly.

The only question that remains is, 'Who are Jesus' brethren?' The Bible clearly places the brethren of Jesus in two categories: those who are related to Him through the Spirit, and those who are related to Him through the flesh.

During a crisis moment in the life of His immediate earthly family, Jesus identified the greater spiritual family of God:

> *'While He was still talking to the multitudes, behold His mother and brothers stood outside, seeking to speak with Him. Then one said to Him, "Look, Your mother and Your brothers are standing outside, seeking to speak with You." But He answered and said to the one who told Him, "Who is My mother and who are My brothers?" And He stretched out His hand toward His disciples and said, "Here are My mother and My brothers! For whoever does the will of My Father in Heaven is My brother and sister and mother."'*
>
> (Matthew 12:46–50)

The 'brethren of Jesus', according to the Lord's own definition, are those who do the will of God the Father. In other words, committed disciples of Messiah. Thus, the true Church of Messiah Jesus is described as the *household* or *family* of God (Ephesians 2:19 and 3:15). Those who are born again of the Spirit of God are *brethren*, *friends*, and *co-heirs* with Jesus!

Spiritual relationship with Jesus takes precedence over any natural or physical affiliation. However, this does not annul Jesus' eternal identification with the Jewish people.

Messiah Jesus was *'born of the seed of David according to the flesh'* (Romans 1:3). He was *'born under the law'* (Galatians 4:4), and grew up as a Jewish child in a Jewish home, surrounded by Jewish customs and Jewish culture. He never disowned or denounced His Jewish heritage. He simply recognized it as a means to an end, and not an end in itself. He was ever mindful of the mission of redemption and of God's love for all men.

Throughout eternity He continues to be known as *'The Lion of the Tribe of Judah'* and *'The Root and the Offspring of David'*, titles that identify Him with the nation of Israel and the Jewish people (Revelation 5:5 and 22:16).

The nations, in this case, are judged on the basis of their treatment of two groups of people: Christians and Jews. It is interesting to note that on many occasions Christians and Jews have been persecuted simultaneously, by the same enemies!

For example, during the notorious Spanish Inquisition of the Fifteenth Century, tens of thousands of innocent people were accused of 'heresy' and were forced to confess their 'sins'. Such confessions were often solicited through harassment, intimidation and torture. The ultimate punishment for 'irreconcilable heretics' was death at the stake.

In many cases, the accused were God-fearing men and women who were disillusioned with the rampant corruption in the Catholic Church, epitomised by the erroneous doctrine and immoral behaviour of the Papacy. New movements such as *The Waldensians* sprang up throughout Europe, seeking to recapture the spirit and truth of primitive Christianity.

Spanish Jewry also suffered enormously during the Inquisition. The demand for the mass conversion of Jews eventually found expression in the ruthless anti-Jewish massacres of 1391, which then led to the Inquisition, and, in 1492, to the ultimatum: 'Convert or be expelled!'

That year, 160,000 Jews left Spain and 20,000 more perished in the search for a new life (over 60,000 had already been killed). Fifty thousand stayed and were baptized, but continued to secretly live as Jews.

Hitler's Third Reich furnished yet another example of the concurrent suffering of Jesus' spiritual and natural brethren. From 1933 to 1939 when war broke out, and during the next six years of tumultuous conflict, the Nazis persecuted and killed Jews simply for being Jews, and Christians who dared to act like true Christians, in an unrestrained display of satanic hatred for God's two Covenant peoples.

Following the Bolshevik Revolution of 1917, and more especially, in the wake of the ascendancy of Joseph Stalin, the

Communist regime discriminated against and actively persecuted two groups of people: Christians and Jews. Various religious groups and ethnic minorities were suppressed by the Soviet authorities, but Christians and Jews suffered the most consistent harassment of all.

The Fundamentalist Islamic Revival which began in Iran in the late 1970s and has subsequently been exported around the world, holds as its avowed goals the destruction of the State of Israel, and the subjugation of the 'infidel nations', meaning the forced conversion or elimination of Christians.

The Woman and Her Offspring

Satan's dual programme of persecution is portrayed in the twelfth chapter of the Book of Revelation:

> *'Now when the dragon saw that he had been cast to the earth, he persecuted the woman who gave birth to the Male Child. But the woman was given two wings of a great eagle, that she might fly into the wilderness to her place, where she is nourished for a time and times and half a time, from the presence of the serpent.*
>
> *So the serpent spewed water out of his mouth like a flood after the woman, that he might cause her to be carried away by the flood. But the earth helped the woman, and the earth opened its mouth and swallowed up the flood which the dragon had spewed out of its mouth.*
>
> *And the dragon was enraged with the woman, and he went to make war with the rest of her offspring, who keep the commandments of God and have the testimony of Jesus Christ.'* (Revelation 12:13–17)

To my mind, this passage of Scripture explains the suffering of both the Jewish people and the Christian Church throughout the past two millenia. Revelation chapter twelve is, in fact, a synopsis of human history from God's perspective.

The Dragon (Satan) is enraged with the Woman (Israel), who

gave birth to the Male Child (Jesus). Satan hates Israel because she is the vehicle of God's redemptive purpose – the channel through which God entered the human family (in the Person of Messiah Jesus) to redeem fallen man from the curse of sin and to reconcile man unto Himself in righteousness.

Satan also hates *'the rest of the Woman's offspring,'* Christian believers, who keep the commandments of God and have the testimony of Messiah Jesus.

Why does Satan hate the witnessing Church? Because the preaching of the Gospel abrogates the power of evil over men and nations; because the testimony of Jesus' followers causes men and women to believe on Him as Saviour and Lord; because the proclamation of the Gospel to all nations precipitates the return of Messiah and the fulness of His Kingdom reign!

At various times in history men have risen up and given tangible expression to Satan's murderous designs. Haman. Antiochus Epiphanes. Ferdinand and Isabella. Semion Petlyura. Stalin. Hitler. Haj Amin al-Husseini. Ayatollah Khomeini. Saddam Hussein. And no doubt there will be more. Eventually the Antichrist, the personification of all evil, will sit in the temple and proclaim himself to be god.

However, God's Word to Abraham's seed, both spiritual and natural, heavenly and earthly, stands sure: *'I will bless those who bless you, and I will curse those who curse you.'* (Genesis 12:3).

And again,

> *'Even the captives of the mighty shall be taken away, and the prey of the terrible be delivered; for I will contend with him who contends with you, and I will save your children. I will feed those who oppress you with their own flesh, and they shall be drunk with their own blood as with sweet wine. All flesh shall know that I, the LORD, am your Saviour, and your Redeemer, the Mighty One of Jacob.'*

(Isaiah 49:25–26)

Furthermore,

> *'Behold, all those who were incensed against you shall be ashamed and disgraced; they shall be as nothing, and those who strive with you shall perish. You shall seek them and not find them – those who contended with you. Those who war against you shall be as nothing, as a non-existent thing. For I, the LORD your God, will hold your hand, saying to you, "Fear not, I will help you."'* (Isaiah 41:11–13)

And finally,

> *'No weapon formed against you shall prosper, and every tongue which rises against you in judgment you shall condemn. This is the heritage of the servants of the LORD, and their righteousness is from Me, says the LORD.'*
> (Isaiah 54:17)

Herein is the patience and faith of the saints, and herein is the Word of the Lord fulfilled:

> *'For the nation and kingdom which will not serve you shall perish, and those nations shall be utterly ruined.'*
> (Isaiah 60:12)

References

1.   *The Prince and the Prophet* by Claude Duvernoy, p. 115.

Chapter 9

Divine Order in the Nations

'Let every soul be subject to the governing authorities. For there is no authority except from God, and the authorities that exist are appointed by God. Therefore whoever resists the authority resists the ordinance of God, and those who resist will bring judgment on themselves.'

(Romans 13:1–2)

The Lord God is not a God of egalitarianism, but of order and structure. Redemptively, all men are equal in God's sight; but functionally, they differ according to God's plan and purpose for their lives. This is true, not only of individuals, but also of nations.

The principle of delegated authority has been established by God, and thus, forms an integral part of the order of creation. Moreover, it is a fundamental law of the Kingdom that governs every area of life.

When there is no respect for this 'chain of command', society is plunged into a whirlpool of violence and confusion.

The principle of delegated authority is revealed in the following spheres: Messiah is the Head of the Church; the husband is the head of the home; employers are the head of employees; the government is the head of the State; pastors/elders are the head of local assemblies, and on an international level, Israel is the head of the nations!

God's choice of a nation to head the family of nations was not based on popular demand; it was not submitted to a vote of men

129

and angels; nor was it derived from a consensus of prophets and sages. It was a unilateral decision, based on God's sovereignty and omniscience.

> *'For thus says the* LORD: *"Sing with gladness for Jacob, and shout among the chief of the nations; proclaim, give praise, and say, 'O* LORD, *save Your people, the remnant of Israel!'"'*
> (Jeremiah 31:7)

The Hebrew word *'rosh'*, translated 'chief', literally means 'head'. As used in the above context, it denotes 'preeminence of place and superiority of rank'. In God's sight, Israel is *Rosh Hauumot*, the head of the nations!

To the Jew First

The principle of Israel's headship over the nations is referred to by the Apostle Paul in his epistle to the Church at Rome.

Speaking of the righteous and impartial judgment of God, Paul declares that God will render to each one according to his deeds:

> *'To those who by patient continuance in doing good seek for glory, honour, and immortality – eternal life; But to those who are self-seeking and do not obey the truth, but obey unrighteousness – indignation and wrath, tribulation and anguish, on every soul of man who does evil, of the Jew first and also of the Greek; But glory, honour and peace to everyone who works what is good, to the Jew first and also to the Greek.'*
> (Romans 2:7–10)

In the Divine order of things, God deals with the Jew first and then with the Gentile. This pattern holds true both in blessing and judgment.

Likewise, Paul declares that *'the Gospel of Jesus Christ is the power of God to salvation for everyone who believes, for the Jew first and also for the Greek'* (Romans 1:16).

Preaching to the Jews in Antioch of Pisidia, Paul and Barnabas boldly exclaimed: *'It was necessary that the Word of God should be spoken to you first; but seeing you reject it, and judge yourselves unworthy of everlasting life, behold, we turn to the Gentiles'* (Acts 13:46).

Describing the signs of His coming and of the end of the age, Jesus said to the disciples, *'Look at the fig tree, and all the trees'* (Luke 21:29).

In Bible symbology, trees are representative of nations or kingdoms. Israel is consistently depicted in the Scriptures as a 'fig tree'.

Thus, we can see the Divine order of nations in Jesus' words, *'The fig tree and all the trees,'* or, *'Israel and all the nations.'*

Parallel Events

Israel is God's prophetic time clock and signal board. When something of great importance takes place in Israel, one should look for an event of corresponding significance in the Church and among the nations.

The events of the twentieth century illustrate the parallel outworking of God's purposes *to the Jew first, and then to the Gentile.*

God's dealings with Israel in **The Balfour Declaration of 1917** coincided with a major revival in the Christian Church, generally referred to as *The Pentecostal Movement*. A new dimension of God's power and glory was restored to the Church as Christians sought for and received the fulness of the Holy Spirit, as promised in the Scriptures.

At the same time tremendous changes were taking place among the nations. The world was plunged into war; the Bolsheviks came to power in Russia, thereby unleashing one of the most oppressive systems of government ever known to man; scientists and inventors ushered mankind into a new era of communication and transportation, as prophesied in Daniel 12:4.

The Rebirth of Israel in 1948 coincided with another significant revival of evangelism and healing in the Church. Household names such as Billy Graham, Oral Roberts and T.L. Osborn commenced their worldwide ministries at that time.

Huge tents and great stadiums were filled with spiritually-hungry people as God moved in a new and powerful way throughout the world.

In the aftermath of another catastrophic war, the United Nations organization was formed; Mao Tse Tung and his communist forces conquered China; and the world entered a new era of nuclear energy, computer technology, and annihilation weaponry.

The Six Day War of 1967 coincided with one of the most significant movements of God in modern Church history. Known as *the Charismatic Renewal*, this worldwide outpouring of the Holy Spirit swept millions of people into the Kingdom of God and released countless multitudes into a new dimension of faith and worship.

The 1973 *Yom Kippur* (Day of Atonement) War signified a fresh dealing of God with pride and sin in Israel, the Church, and the nations.

Over sixty heads of State changed within eighteen months, mainly because of the exposure of corruption and sin. The most notable of these changes occurred in the USA, where the infamous *Watergate Scandal* eventually forced the resignation of President Richard Nixon.

The 1982 Peace for Galilee War which drove the PLO out of Southern Lebanon and secured Israel's northern townships from terrorist attacks also had its counterpart in the Church.

The Charismatic/Pentecostal movement, which for almost ten years had been plagued by division and sectarianism, experienced a significant outpouring of healing and reconciliation, which, in turn, gave birth to a new move of God's Spirit in the Church.

In November, 1987, the Palestinian uprising commenced in the Gaza Strip. Popularly referred to as **The Intifada**, this mass uprising was and continues to be incited and orchestrated by hardline Islamic fundamentalists who care little about the plight of the Palestinians, but willingly use them as pawns in a strategy to checkmate Israel.

The Intifada also has its correlative in the Church and among the nations. There is an increasing spirit of lawlessness, rebellion and anarchy in the world. Almost every day reports come to hand of revolutions, uprisings, ethnic conflicts, civil disturbances, coup d'etats and wars. Some are legitimate expressions of revolt against ungodly and repressive regimes. Others are simply expressions of rebellion against the principle of authority and government.

Many pastors and church leaders have testified of a marked increase in the level of spiritual warfare since 1988. In nation after nation, believers are experiencing a mounting intensity in the battle against the powers of darkness.

Exodus II, the immigration of Soviet Jews to Israel, is unfolding simultaneously with a remarkable transformation in the spiritual, political and social constitution of Eastern Europe.

After generations of enslavement to a godless communist system, many nations are now enjoying the first taste of political, cultural and religious freedom. Central to and undergirding this amazing revolution is a major revival of Christianity. Disillusioned with the failure of Communism and Marxist ideology, tens of thousands of people are turning to Jesus Christ and the Bible for answers.

Emboldened by the Holy Spirit and the opportunity of the moment, Christian believers are proclaiming the Gospel wherever and whenever they can – in churches, in factories, in the streets, in marketplaces, and from house to house.

A Blessing to the Nations

The purpose of God for the nations is clearly portrayed in the nineteenth chapter of the prophet Isaiah. Here we see the judgment of God against the idols of Egypt and the humbling of that nation before the Lord. Yet judgment gives way to mercy as Egypt turns to worship the One True God:

> '*In that day there will be an altar to the LORD in the midst of the land of Egypt, and a pillar to the LORD at its border. And it will be for a sign and for a witness to the LORD of hosts in the land of Egypt; for they will cry to the LORD because of the oppressors, and He will send them a Saviour and a Mighty One, and He will deliver them.*

> *Then the* LORD *will be known to Egypt, and the Egyptians will know the* LORD *in that day, and will make sacrifice and offering; yes, they will make a vow to the* LORD *and perform it. And the* LORD *will strike Egypt, He will strike and heal it; they will return to the* LORD, *and He will be entreated by them and heal them.'*   (Isaiah 19:19–22)

'God so loved the world' is a central theme of the Bible. In considering God's purpose for Israel, one should not lose sight of the ultimate purpose of His Kingdom: to redeem all nations and to fill the whole earth with His glory!

Divine order in the nations decrees that God's dealings are with the Jew first and then with the Gentile. However, there is no partiality with God. Israel, like the Church, is a means to an end and not an end in itself.

Israel, blessed of God, is to be a blessing to all nations – a fact borne out by the words of Isaiah:

> *'In that day Egypt and Iraq* (Assyria) *will be connected by a highway. And the Egyptians and the Iraqi will move freely backwards and forwards between their lands, and they shall worship the same God. And Israel will be their ally; the three will be together, and Israel will be a blessing to them. For the Lord will bless Egypt and Iraq because of their friendship with Israel. He will say, "Blessed be Egypt, My people; blessed be Iraq, the land I have made; blessed be Israel, My inheritance!"'*   (Isaiah 19:23–25, TLB)

To seek Israel's destruction is to sign one's own death warrant! To the extent that a nation fights against the purposes of God, to that same extent it will be judged and humiliated.

But to all who recognize and accept God's purpose in Israel, the Jewish State will become a channel of blessing from the Lord of hosts!

Chapter 10

The Real Conflict in the Middle East

'Put on the whole armour of God, that you may be able to stand against the wiles (schemings) of the devil. For we do not wrestle against flesh and blood, but against principalities, against powers, against spiritual hosts of wickedness in heavenly places. Therefore take up the whole armour of God, that you may be able to withstand in the evil day, and having done all, to stand.' (Ephesians 6:11–13)

The real issue in the Middle East is not political, social, economic or racial: it is spiritual. Israel is in the forefront of a conflict between the Word of God and the principalities of Humanism and Islam.

To understand the nature of the confrontation, one must look beyond the suave and subtle speeches of politicians and powerbrokers, the fanatical proclamations of maniacal warlords and terrorist leaders, and the distorted and deceitful reports of the news media.

The real battle is in the spiritual realm, otherwise known as *heavenly places*. The conflict on earth, involving flesh and blood, is simply a reflection of the battle that is raging in the spirit world.

Satan hates Israel because of her integral role in the fulfilment of God's purposes – past, present and future. From the moment God said, *'The Seed of the woman will bruise the serpent's head'* (that is, cancel Satan's dominion), there has been enmity between the serpent and the woman (Genesis 3:15).

The Woman is the nation of Israel – the vehicle through which God entered the human family as a Man. *The Seed* is Jesus the Messiah, and by extension, His Body the Church.

Through His death and resurrection, Jesus destroyed him who had the power of death, that is, the devil (Hebrews 2:14). Furthermore, disciples of Jesus are authorized to *cast out demons* in His Name, and to set people free from the tyranny of darkness (Mark 16:17).

From the murder of Abel in the fields of Eden (Genesis 4:8) to the slaughter of the innocents in Bethlehem (Matthew 2:16), Satan attempted to identify and destroy *The Seed*. If he had succeeded in destroying the Seed or the vehicle bearing the Seed, the Plan of Redemption and the establishment of God's Kingdom would have been thwarted. But thank God, *The Lion of the Tribe of Judah* prevailed to open the Scroll of Redemption!

The successful birth of the Messiah did not mean, however, the end of Israel's usefulness in the plan and purpose of God. The prophecies of Isaiah, Jeremiah, and the Apostle Paul indicate a special end-time assignment for the Jewish people. Indeed, the restoration of national Israel signals *the beginning of the end* of God's programme for this present age!

Israel has an important part to play in the Second Advent of Messiah. The outpouring of the Holy Spirit upon the Jewish people will consummate the last great move of God in the earth. The glory of God will be revealed through Israel in a way that will affect all nations. And it is to the holy city of Jerusalem, the restored capital of a sovereign Jewish State, that Messiah Jesus will return as King of kings and Lord of lords.

Satan knows that to destroy Israel would be to thwart the fulfilment of God's prophetic Word and Kingdom purpose. To put it simply, if there was no nation of Israel, no city of Jerusalem, and no Jewish people, then the Lord would have 'nowhere to lay His head' – no place to which He could return.

In my opinion, there is a greater concentration of spiritual forces in the Middle East than in any other region of the world.

Jerusalem is indeed, 'the centre of the earth', geographically, politically and spiritually!

Over the years I have visited and ministered in a number of major cities and have encountered various levels of spiritual conflict. But I have never witnessed as intense a battle as in the heavenly places over Jerusalem.

Wherever one turns there is visible evidence of the quest for spiritual supremacy: mosques, churches, synagogues, UN representatives, Palestinian activists, etc.

The invisible war is all about two kingdoms and two spirits: the Kingdom of God and His Holy Spirit, and the kingdom of darkness and the spirit of antichrist. The Kingdom of God is principally represented in the Middle East by the true Church (the Body of Messiah), and in an extraordinary sense by the nation of Israel.

The kingdom of darkness is principally represented in the Middle East by the forces of religious and secular humanism, and the religion of Islam.

Principality of Humanism

The prophecy of Zechariah graphically describes the age-old conflict between humanism and the Kingdom of God:

> 'For I have bent Judah, My bow, fitted the bow with Ephraim, and raised up your sons, O Zion, against your sons, O Greece, and made you like the sword of a mighty man.'
> (Zechariah 9:13)

The word *Zion* is used in the Scriptures to denote the City of God. Historically, it refers to a hilly area in the eastern part of Jerusalem which David conquered and made the capital of his kingdom, and where he pitched a tent for the Ark of the Covenant.

The Ark represented the Throne of God in the midst of His people, and was constantly attended by worshipping Levites specially commissioned to commemorate, thank and praise the Lord God of Israel.

Zion, therefore, bespeaks Divine order and rulership, and the establishment of God's Kingdom on earth.

Greece, on the other hand, represents the nations outside the Covenant – *Gentiles*, who are without the true knowledge of God.

Moreover, *Greece* represents that philosophy and worldview which places man at the centre of the universe, declaring him to be master of his own destiny and the measure of all things!

The modern humanistic worldview is by and large a product of ancient Greek philosophy. **Heraclitus of Ephesus** was one of the first Greek philosophers ever recorded. Born in about 535 BC, Heraclitus is credited as the founder of an independent metaphysical system that enunciated, as the principle of the universe, 'Becoming', thus implying that everything is and at the same time, and in the same relation, is not.

Heraclitus denied the reality of Being, and declared Becoming, or eternal flux and change, to be the sole reality. He espoused the physical doctrine that all phenomena are in a state of continuous transition from non-existence to existence, and vice versa – 'everything is and is not', all things are, and nothing remains.

Heraclitus selected fire, according to him the most complete embodiment of the process of Becoming, as the principle of empirical existence, out of which all things, including even the soul, grow by way of a quasi condensation, and into which all things must in course of time be again resolved. But this primordial fire is in itself that Divine rational process, the harmony of which constitutes the law of the universe.

According to Heraclitus, real knowledge constitutes a comprehending of this all pervading harmony as embodied in the manifold of perception, and real virtue consisting in the subordination of the individual to the laws of this harmony, as the universal reason where true freedom alone is to be found.

Heraclitus taught that the soul approaches most nearly to perfection when it is most akin to the fiery vapour out of which it was originally created, and as this is most so in death, 'while we live our souls are dead in us, but when we die our souls are restored to life.'

The few surviving statements of Heraclitus eloquently express the philosophy of modern humanism, most notably his assertion that 'everything flows', that is, everything is in a state of flux; and 'a person cannot step into the same river twice.'

The philosophy of humanism takes human experience as the starting point for man's knowledge of himself and the work of God and nature. It denies the biblical doctrine of the sinful nature of humanity and emphasizes the inherent worth and dignity of every person. It rejects not only the moral absolutes of the Bible, but the very notion of a Personal God, a Sovereign Creator, to Whom we must give account.

For example, **Protagoras of Abdera**, the first of the so-called Greek Sophists (481–411 BC), argued in a treatise entitled *Truth*, that if all things are in flux, so that sensation is subjective, it follows that 'man is the measure of all things, of what is, that it is, and of what is not, that it is not.' In other words, there is no such thing as objective truth!

Few Christians realize the extent of humanistic influence in today's society. Like an octopus from the nether world, humanism has spread its tentacles into every strata of man's existence. The *World Book Encyclopedia* succinctly states: 'Much of modern western culture comes from humanistic achievements. The spirit and goals of humanism still influence the arts, education and government.'

Most, if not all of the world's leading policy-makers and behind the scenes power-brokers are imbued with the philosophy of humanism.

However, the essential nature of humanism is not philosophical or ideological, but spiritual. Humanism is a spirit from Hell, sent forth to deceive mankind into serving and worshipping the creature, rather than the Creator (Romans 1:25).

The principality of humanism made its first appearance in the Garden of Eden when man, striving to be God, ate of the forbidden fruit. It reached the zenith of its influence in the ancient world under the leadership of Nimrod, who supervised the building of the Tower of Babel, a monument to human pride and self-rule (Genesis 11). And its deception will be consummated in the person of the Antichrist, who will oppose and exalt himself above all that is called God or that is worshipped, and will sit in the temple of God and proclaim himself as God! (2 Thessalonians 2:4).

The Kings of the Earth

It should come as no surprise when humanistic organizations that refute the existence of God and the authority of His Word also deny Israel the right to exist within sovereign and secure borders in her Divinely-appointed homeland.

A case in point is the 1947 United Nations plan to 'internationalize' the city of Jerusalem. The plan was ostensibly conceived to protect religious and historical sites, and to guarantee freedom of access to Jews, Moslems and Christians. But in reality, it was a direct fulfilment of Psalm two: *The kings of the earth taking their stand against the Lord and His Messiah;* natural-minded men seeking to usurp Divine authority and install their own 'king' in Zion.

The ultimate imposition of the spirit and philosophy of humanism on Israel is described by the prophet Zechariah: *'And it shall happen in that day that I will make Jerusalem a very heavy stone for all peoples; all who would heave it away will surely be cut in pieces, though all nations of the earth are gathered against it'* (Zechariah 12:3).

The Hebrew word *'goyim'*, translated 'nations', denotes Gentiles who are aliens from the commonwealth of Israel, strangers from the covenants of promise and without the hope of Messiah, and by implication, *worshippers of false gods and/or adherents of a secular humanistic worldview*.

Israel's war with the principality of humanism is being waged on the religious front as well. There are two churches emerging in the earth: the true Church, the Body of Messiah, comprising all born again, Spirit-filled believers, regardless of race, colour or denomination; and the false Church, described in the Book of Revelation as *The Great Harlot* and *Mystery Babylon*.

I do not believe that the false Church is represented by any one particular denomination. Rather, it consists of all who claim to be 'Christian', hold to a form of external piety, but deny the life-changing power of the Cross of Jesus. This kind of 'social Christianity' or 'religion of tolerance' is rampant in some of the mainline denominations, but has no place in the Kingdom of Heaven.

Higher Criticism of the Bible, Liberation Theology, and Ecumenism are all manifestations of religious humanism. The signs of apostasy are everywhere to be seen: Unregenerate bishops denying the virgin birth and physical resurrection of Messiah; liberal theologians rejecting the inspiration and inerrancy of Scripture; backslidden churches condoning abortion, ordaining homosexuals and espousing licentiousness.

A logical extension of such religious heresy is the rejection of Israel. If one does not respect the authority of God's Word, how can one possibly respect or even recognize its prophetic fulfilment in modern day Israel?

Ultimately, the forces of religious and secular humanism will converge under the headship of the False Prophet, who, in turn, will direct men to worship the Antichrist, also known in Scripture as the *Man of Sin* and *the Beast*. Not surprisingly, one of his secret and determined goals will be the destruction of Israel.

Principality of Islam

The history of Islam dates back to 610 AD, when a spirit being, claiming to be the Archangel Gabriel, appeared to an illiterate caravan trader as he was meditating in a cave near the city of Mecca. The man's name was Mohammed, and he was commanded to 'recite' the words that he heard.

The angel gave Mohammed revelation from God to correct 'all that the Jews had corrupted in the Old Testament' and 'all that the Christians had corrupted in the New Testament'. The revelation was subsequently recorded in *the Koran* – the Writings – which, together with the *Sunna* or *Hadith* – the sayings of the prophet – constitutes the *Shari'a* – the Law of Islam.

Three years later, Mohammed stood in Mecca and proclaimed the revelations he had received from 'Gabriel' or *Jibril*. He denounced the polytheistic idolatry centred around the strange cube of black rock called the *Kaaba* (which some scholars believe to be a meteorite), and promulgated the worship of the one true God named *Allah*, who, incidentally, was the patron deity of the stone in the old pagan *Kaaba* religion.

Mohammed later laid claim to the *Kaaba* as an Islamic shrine. To this day, Moslems throughout the world turn and face the *Kaaba Shrine* and recite their prayers, and millions make the *Haj* pilgrimage to this most hallowed place in Islamic lore.

Islamic theology teaches that God first revealed Himself to the Jews and they committed the revelation to writing in the Old Testament. But the Jews corrupted the revelation God gave them. They misinterpreted and twisted it to their own ends, so God turned away from them and embraced a new group of people, the Christians.

He began to reveal Himself to the Christians and they likewise committed the revelation to writing in the New Testament. But like the Jews, they corrupted the revelation and perverted it to their own ends. So God turned His back on the Christians. He finished with the Jews and finished with the Christians, and turned instead to Mohammed. Thus, Mohammed is God's final and most sublime prophet, and the Koran is God's final and complete revelation.

In the words of the *Shahada*, the Islamic Affirmation of Faith, 'There is no God but Allah, and Mohammed is his prophet.' The word *'Islam'* in Arabic means 'submission'. In the eyes of its followers, Islam is predestined to bring all nations into subjection to Allah, and his prophet Mohammed.

To this end, the Koran calls for Moslems to wage *jihad* or holy war against all unbelievers, especially Christians and Jews. Martyrdom in the course of *jihad* is rewarded with immediate access to Paradise, which, according to the Koran, is a place of extravagant sensual pleasure.

By guaranteeing eternal life and paradise to all who die in the cause of Islam, Mohammed whipped his Bedouin followers to a frenzy. Their bloody, warlike excursions, which were actually nothing more than the same marauding raids they had been accustomed to for centuries, now had a religious pretext and a Divine sanction. Empowered by the spirit of *Jihad*, Moslem warriors quickly advanced upon the Middle East.

Within a few short years they gained control of the whole Arabian Peninsular. Entire communities of Jews and Christians were either forcibly converted to Islam, promptly expelled or brutally executed. The 'religion of the sword' brooked no dissension.

Shortly after Mohammed's death in 632 AD, Palestine and Syria capitulated to Islamic might. The march of Islam continued into Central Asia, conquering Iran, Afghanistan and Northwestern India. Islam also turned its attention to Egypt, one of the major Christian centres of the Seventh Century. In a few short years, thousands of Christians were slaughtered or forced to flee. Islam took the whole of Egypt, leaving only a small minority Coptic Church.

An unsuccessful revolt in 722 AD incurred the full wrath of Islamic law. Monks were branded in the head, civilians oppressed with heavy taxation, churches demolished, pictures and crosses destroyed, and a few years later, all Copts were also branded.

The Islamic Revolution swept through North Africa and reached Carthage, the other great Christian centre, wiping it out in its entirety.

Observing the sorry condition of the Eastern Church at the time of the Islamic revolution, one handbook of Christian history states:

'By this time the Christian religion was six hundred years old, and all through the East it had decayed terribly. The Eastern Church had split into innumerable sects, all quarrelling fiercely with one another. Its intellectual activity had become a barren controversy about theological subtleties, which utterly obscured the plain facts of the Gospel. Its worship was an elaborate ritual, with a use of images not easy to distinguish from idol-worship. It had forgotten its earlier enthusiasm for missionary enterprise. In a word, Eastern Christianity had lost its sense of God.'[1]

Following the conquest of North Africa, Moslem armies crossed the Strait of Gibraltar, capturing much of Portugal and

Spain. Then, crossing the Pyrenees mountains, they successfully penetrated the Southern part of Frankish Gaul.

Finally, in 732 AD, the march of Islam came to a halt at a town called **Tours**, two hundred kilometres from Paris. There, by the grace of God, the very weak Christian forces under the leadership of Charles Martel met and conquered the enormously superior Moslem forces.

Many historians regard this battle, which began at Tours and ended at **Poitiers**, as one of the most important ever fought, because it determined that Christianity, rather than Islam, would dominate Europe. Islam was flung back to Spain, where it remained for another four centuries, until it was driven out of there into North Africa.

Following the death of Mohammed and his successors, Moslem leaders became convinced of the need to moderate Islamic policy toward minority groups – a policy that often resulted in mass murder or forced conversion.

The Dhimmi People

Christians and Jews who refused to convert to Islam were subject to *dhimmi* status in Moslem society. They were regarded as second-class citizens with restricted rights and privileges, or simply treated as slaves.

The Christian Mid-East Conference Fact Page notes that under Moslem rule, Christians and Jews were forced to pay oppressive taxes and fees. One of these, the *Kharaj*, was similar to the 'protection money' that mobsters demand of those they want to terrify. It was the 'offer they could not refuse'. Should the fee be lacking, the victim would be exposed to vicious attacks.

The *Jizya* was another tax that Christians and Jews were forced to pay at a humiliating public ceremony at which they were struck on the head or the neck. In addition, they had to wear the receipt around the neck or wrist; without it they could be jailed at will.

Christians and Jews were not allowed to testify against Moslems; in fact, Islamic courts refused to accept evidence from Christians and Jews on the grounds that they were 'of a perverse and mendacious character', because they supposedly 'denied the superiority of Islam'. Christians and Jews were also forbidden to give orders to Moslems in work, or to exercise authority over them in any way.

Moreover, Christians and Jews were forbidden to marry Moslems, although Moslems could marry whomever they pleased. They were also forbidden to carry arms or protect themselves, to perform religious practices in public, or to build new houses of worship.

As a further humiliation, Christians and Jews were not permitted to ride horses or camels in public, and in some cases, even donkeys; further, they had to dismount and abase themselves before passing Moslems.

They were not allowed to congregate and talk in the street, and had to walk with their eyes lowered when passing Moslems. They could speak to Moslems only when authorized to do so, and were told to lower their voices. In their shops, they were sometimes forced to crouch so that Moslem clients would see only their heads and not their bodies.

To add insult to injury, Christians and Jews were sometimes forced to wear distinctive clothing for identification, and to maintain their homes and businesses in a way that would be immediately recognized.

While Christian and Jewish communities were in some cases permitted to remain in Moslem societies, they were subject to constant attack. Their homes and businesses were looted and vandalized, and their churches and synagogues were pillaged, burned, or completely destroyed.

Christians and Jews were never allowed to worship freely in Moslem lands. The ringing of bells, crosses, icons, banners, and all other religious objects were prohibited.[2]

In summary, 'unbelievers' in a Moslem society were at best tolerated, albeit in a climate of discrimination and repression; and at worst, forcibly converted, expelled or destroyed.

Islam Rides Again

Islam launched another attempt to conquer the world in the Fifteenth century. Conquests in the Balkans and Asia Minor

were temporarily halted by Tamerlane, but by 1444 the Ottoman Turks were firmly in control of Eastern Europe.

On May 29th, 1453, Ottoman armies captured **Constan-
tinople**, and made it the capital of their burgeoning empire. The
Crimea, Greece, Syria, and then the Marmelukes of Egypt
were swept into the Turkish net, and by 1520 **Selim I** was able to
proclaim himself *Caliph* of the entire Moslem world.

But it was his son and successor, **Suleiman I**, known to the
West as **Suleiman the Magnificent**, who posed the greatest
threat to Christendom. Having invaded and conquered Hungary, Suleiman advanced upon Vienna. On September 27th,
1529, the vast Turkish host laid siege to the capital of the
German Empire, which, at that time, was being swept by the
fires of Lutheran revival.

Interestingly enough, it was in the self-same year of 1529, at
the Diet of Speyer, that Emperor Charles V attempted to curb
Luther's movement by force. But some of the princes of the
German states stood up in 'protest', which led to the movement
being called *Protestant*. From that point on, the movement
separated itself from Catholicism and became known as *The
Reformation*.

One can only wonder what might have happened to the
Reformation, and indeed, to the Christian Church, if Suleiman
had succeeded in taking Vienna. To my mind, an Islamic
onslaught on the German Empire at the very time of spiritual
renewal was, quite clearly, an attempt by the powers of darkness to abort God's programme of restoration in the Church.

But through the grace of God, the city, the empire, and the
fledgling revival were spared. On the 14th day of October, after
a most desperate assault that lasted for four days, the invaders
were compelled to retire, leaving Vienna in possession of its
heroic defenders, led most gallantly by Nicholas Von Salm.

Vienna's respite, however, was relatively short-lived. A little
over 150 years later, in the summer of 1683, **Kara Mustafa**, the
ambitious Grand Vizier of Turkey, marched with an enormous
army of almost 500,000 men against the Austrian capital. His
pet scheme was the conquest of Germany, which, as we have
noted, was the birthplace of the Reformation.

Emperor Leopold fled Vienna with his court, and was quickly followed by the wealthier inhabitants of the city. Command of the capital passed into the hands of **Count Rudiger Von Starhemberg**, who mobilized all classes of people – including the priests and the women – to labour diligently at the fortifications.

At sunrise on July 14th, the Moslem hordes arrived at the gates of Vienna, leaving behind them a trail of burning cottages and desolated villages. The Moslem camp arranged itself in the form of a crescent. Splendid above all things was the tent of the Grand Vizier, made of green silk, worked with gold and silver, set with precious stones, and containing inside the holy standard of the prophet.

The next two months were the most difficult imaginable for the besieged inhabitants of Vienna. Fire broke out in the city, being scarcely extinguished; disease raged among the people, owing to the long confinement in close quarters and an enforced diet of chiefly salt meat.

In desperation, Emperor Leopold solicited the help of the King of Poland, **John Sobieski**, and all Europe now looked to him as its saviour.

Polish and German forces joined arms at **Krems** on the Danube, near Vienna – 77,000 men ready for active operations on the field, but still outnumbered approximately six to one by the Ottoman army.

On September 12th, after Mass, Sobieski descended from the city to encounter the masses of Moslems in the plains below. Before the battle, the King knighted his son and made a patriotic address to his troops, in which he told them that on this occasion, they were not defending Vienna alone, but rather all Christendom, and that they were not fighting for an earthly sovereign, but for the King of kings!

The shouts of the Polish and German soldiers bore to the enemy the dreaded name of **Sobieski**, familiar to them on many a well-fought field. The assault was made simultaneously on the wings and the centre of the enemy's ranks. In spite of the bravery of the Turks, they were overpowered by the *elan* of the Poles.

Realizing that defeat was inevitable, the Grand Vizier fled

with a remnant of his army. After the rout was completed and an immense booty was captured, Sobieski and his troops entered Vienna. Divine Service was performed in St. Stephen's Cathedral, with a priest reading aloud from the text, *'There was a man sent from God, whose name was John.'*

Few Christians realize just how close Europe came to being totally dominated by Islam. If Islam had succeeded in gaining control of 'Christian' Europe, there could quite conceivably have been no Moravian Revival in Germany, and hence, no Evangelical or Wesleyan Revival in England.

The Oil Gun

Following its defeat in 1683, Islam retired to the Middle East and remained in stagnation until the Twentieth Century. Then, two things happened: Firstly, the Jews began to return to *Eretz* Israel in large numbers and to upset the demographic and geopolitical *status quo* of the Middle East; and secondly, Islam discovered oil within its territory.

Islamic leaders believe that Allah gave them oil so as to enable them to win back what they lost militarily. Western politicians and industrialists may have little interest in Islamic theology, but they are extremely concerned about a precious commodity called **oil**. The discovery of oil has given Islam a bargaining chip, or more literally, a weapon of extortion with which to intimidate the Western 'infidels'.

There are two important facts about Islam that Christians need to understand.

Firstly, Islam is a false religious system that denies the deity of the Lord Jesus and the validity of His redemptive work, the authority of the Word of God as constituted in the Old and New Testaments, and the existence of the nation of Israel.

Following are some of the main points on which the teaching of Islam contradicts that of the Bible:

1. The Bible declares that Jesus is the Eternal Son of God. Islam declares that God has no son, and rejects the concept of One God revealed in Three Persons.

   In fact, those who declare that Jesus is the Son of God

are 'unbelievers' who will be 'forbidden entrance into Paradise, and shall be cast into the fire of hell', for 'the Messiah, the son of Mary, was no more than an apostle' (Sura 5:73–75).

In the place where Solomon built the temple and God caused His glorious Name to dwell, there now stands a golden-domed mosque. Inscribed on its ceramic tiles are these words from the Koran: 'Give to God alone the glory. God has no son. God does not need a friend or a companion. Do not say that He has a son. Give to God alone the glory.'

For this reason, Christians of the Middle Ages called the Mosque 'the abomination of desolation', standing where it ought not to stand.

2.   The Bible declares that Jesus literally died on the Cross for our sins and literally rose from the dead on the third day. Islam admits that Jesus lived, taught and worked miracles, but contends that He did not die – rather, He was translated to the right hand of God and an embodied spirit resembling Him appeared to undergo crucifixion.

However, if Jesus did not die, then there is no remission of sin (Hebrews 9:22). And if there is no remission of sin, then there is no hope of righteousness or of eternal life. If there is no death, then there is no resurrection, and if there is no resurrection, then there is no hope of being born again (1 Peter 1:3).

3.   The Bible declares that Jesus will actually return to earth at the consummation of the age, to judge the world in righteousness as King of Kings and Lord of Lords.

Islam admits that Jesus will return to earth just before the Day of Judgment, but in order to proclaim that Mohammed is God's final and most sublime prophet, and to lead all of mankind into Islam. Then the 'son of Mary' will die like an ordinary man, and be resurrected with everyone else on the last day.

4.   The Bible declares that Jesus is the fulfilment of the Law and the Prophets (Matthew 5:17), the complete and ultimate revelation of God (Hebrews 1:2), the fulness of God in bodily form (Colossians 2:9).

Islam declares that it alone is the fulfilment of the revelation contained in the Old and New Testaments, and that Mohammed is the greatest of all prophets.

5. In the Bible, Jesus promised His disciples that He would send them another *Helper* to be with them and in them (John 14:16–17). This promise was fulfilled through the outpouring of the Holy Spirit on the Day of Pentecost.

   Islam, however, claims that Mohammed is the promised *Comforter*, or *Helper*.

6. The Bible declares that Abraham offered his son Isaac on the altar on Mount Moriah, and received him back from the dead in a figurative sense (Genesis 22:9–13).

   Islam declares that Ishmael, not Isaac, was offered up to God, and that the sacrifice took place at the *Kaaba Shrine* in Mecca. Abraham, whom the New Testament calls *'the father of the faithful'*, is revered as the first Moslem.

7. The Bible declares the Church to be the Body of Messiah – the house, the temple, and the inheritance of God. The Bible also declares the Jewish people to be beloved in the sight of God, and that through the mercy and covenant faithfulness of God, they will be regathered to the Land and grafted back into the Body of Messiah.

   Islam, however, repudiates both the Christian Church and the Jewish nation, declaring that God has finished with them both. 'There is no God but Allah, Mohammed is his prophet, and Islam is the one true religion, the completion of all that God began to do through Jews and Christians.'

Secondly, Islam is bent on world conquest. It has an insatiable desire to rule the world, and will be satisfied with nothing less than absolute dominion. Hence, it is impossible for evangelical Christianity and fundamentalist Islam to co-exist.

According to the *Shari'a* the world is divided into *dar al-harb* (the city of war) and *dar al-Islam* (the city of Islam). The latter is that area which is already actually governed according to the *Shari'a*. The city of war is 'that which is not, but which, actually or potentially, is a seat of war for Moslems until by conquest it is turned into "Abode of Islam".'

By nature, Islam is militant and coercive, and has often

resorted to violence in order to obtain the 'submission' of non-believers. The present wave of fundamentalist terrorist attacks in Western capitals, as well as in Israel itself, is but a practical application of Islamic theology.

For example, in Sura 8:39, the Koran urges all Moslems to 'make war' on unbelievers 'until idolatry is no more and Allah's religion reigns supreme.'

And in the words of Middle East historian, Professor P.J. Vatikiotis: 'Islam demands that its adherents make every effort so that Islamic law reigns supreme, until it controls the entire world.'

The Arabic word for peace, *'salaam'*, means 'to submit'. Thus, the Moslem view of 'peace' is a world totally dominated by and submissive to the rule of Islam. It would behove us to remember this point as we watch the 'peace process' unfold in the Middle East!

A recent interview with Jamil Hamami, a senior local activist of the radical *Hamas* movement, reveals a classic Islamic fundamentalist worldview:

'"Palestine is Islamic land in its entirety, and it is impossible to concede any part of it. Neither the PLO nor any Arab state has the authority to make concessions with regard to Palestinian soil." The only political solution, according to Hamami, is the establishment of an Islamic state in all of Palestine, which would become part of a larger Islamic state that would ultimately encompass the world. "The solution for us, the Jews and all of humanity is Islam," he declared.

Partition, for Hamami, is out of the question. "There is room for only one state in Palestine, from the river to the sea," he said. "...the aim is to impose political 'pragmatism' on the Palestinians and prevent an Islamic reawakening," he said. "It's a religious struggle between Islam and non-Islamic nations, who are trying to stop the Islamic trend in the region. Islam will win in the end," Hamami summed up. "The future belongs to religion. All the other ideologies have failed. The Islamic trend is growing, and I hope it continues to gain. Islam seeks prosperity for all humanity.'''[3]

Similarly, the *Islamic Jihad*, another hardline, fundamentalist movement, defines the Palestinian problem as an 'Islamic, not a national (wataniyya) problem concerning the Palestinians, nor an all-Arab (qawmiyya) problem concerning the Arabs. It is the problem of the "Islamic nation" in its entirety, whether considered from the point of view of history or from that of "sound" Koranic consciousness.'

The *intifada*, according to the *Islamic Jihad*, is an 'Islamic revolution to liberate all of Palestine.'[4]

However, it is not just Israel that is in Islam's sights, but the whole of the 'Christian' West. A Moslem booklet, entitled *Moslem-Christian Alliance*, published in Istanbul, makes a strong case for Moslem-Christian friendship and inter-faith dialogue.

'Moreover, the Saying of the Prophet Mohammed further states that in the end of time, true, pious, devout Christians will unite with Moslems and put a great fight together against the common threat, Atheism. For the time being, true devout Moslems must unite not only with their co-religionists, colleagues and fellow brothers, but with true Christian believers...'

However, the booklet goes on to show that the real aim of 'friendship and cooperation' is not peaceful **co-existence**, but **conquest**.

'Eventually, Christianity will be purified and get rid of all superstitions and misbeliefs, and will unite with the true Islamic Religion. Thereby Christianity will be in a way transformed into Islam, and by adopting guidance from the Koran, the Christian community will become a follower of Islam and Islam Religion will be the leader position (sic). The true religion of Islam will gain a great power as a result of that unification.'

Through large-scale immigration, significant financial invest-
ment and property acquisition, and vigorous proselytisation,
Islam is successfully infiltrating and subverting the quasi-
Christian citadels of Europe and North America.

There are already some seven million Moslems in Western
Europe, and the number is constantly growing. A similar picture emerges in the USA, where it is estimated that in a few
more years Islam will be the third largest religious denomination, replacing Judaism, which has held that place since the
1880s.

On the outskirts of Rome, the seat of Roman Catholicism,
there now stands a huge $30-million mosque. Over the last
decade and a half, the number of mosques in Britain has
increased dramatically – from 150 to over 1,100 – many of them
being former church buildings. In Brussels, the world centre for
the European Economic Community, there are more mosques
than churches.

In Israel itself, Moslem fundamentalists are exerting enormous pressure on Arab Christians to convert to Islam and/or
join the uprising against Israeli rule. Most Moslem Arabs
believe it is a contradiction in terms to be both Arab and
Christian, since they equate Arabism with Islam.

An objective observer cannot help but see that Christians live
in fear of Moslems in the Middle East, and many are opting to
emigrate from the area which was the birthplace and cradle of
Christianity. Ironically, even the 'Christian quarter' of the Old
City of Jerusalem is no longer Christian, since it has a Moslem
majority.

Writing in the November/December (1992) issue of *Terra
Santa*, an organ of the Roman Catholic Franciscan order,
Father Georges Abou-Khazen of Bethlehem said that the emigration of Arab Christians from the country is the result of
pressure from Moslems, although most local Christian leaders
have blamed the Israeli occupation for the phenomenon.

Abou-Khazen said that Moslems, frustrated by the demographic, social and legal realities, are seeking to *Islamicize* the
Land, and to this end, considerable sums have been contributed
by the Moslem states. Moreover, he concluded that 'in the

Moslem world there cannot be, in the near future, a pluralistic or democratic society.'

'The Last Attempt of Satan'

On May 14th, 1948, the unthinkable and the impossible actually happened: a Jewish State arose in the very heartland of Islam.

The rebirth of Israel is nothing less than a slap in the face of Islamic theology. It is a refutation of both Mohammed and the Koran, and a visible, tangible 'thorn in the flesh' of Moslem expansionism. Furthermore, it is proof-positive of the veracity of the Old and New Testaments.

The late Ayatollah Khomeini, architect of the Iranian revolution, described Israel as 'the last attempt of Satan to frustrate the triumph of Islam'. The principality of Islam does indeed have a controversy with Zion!

The Islamic message concerning the Jews and their destiny is quite clear: the Jews are destined to be persecuted, humiliated and tortured forever, and it is a Moslem duty to see to it that they are persecuted, tortured and humiliated.

Islamic tradition, ascribed to Mohammed, insists that 'Islam is superior, nothing can be superior over it.' This means that Islam has been destined to rule and that a Moslem should never be in subjection to non-Moslems. The establishment of the State of Israel thus broke every single Islamic rule governing Islamic territory, Islamic holy places, and the legal position of the Jew in Islamic law.

The establishment of the State of Israel is regarded by Moslems as a reverse of history, an abnormal phenomenon in which the Jew rules over the Moslem, and a negation of the Divine Word. Therefore, it is the duty of every Moslem to correct this aberration.

In Islamic tradition, God's Kingdom will arrive and be established only after the Moslems kill all the Jews. Consequently, the reappearance of the Jews as an independent, strong, proud national and political entity is a fact that Islam finds impossible to accept. To Moslems, the existence of a Jewish State is nothing short of a cosmic catastrophe.

Behind all the talk of human rights, occupied territories, Israeli aggression etc. is the hatred of Islam for God's Ancient Covenant People. It is not a hatred that can be easily understood by Western-minded politicians, for it is rooted in the spiritual realm – in the opposition of the powers of darkness to the establishment of God's Kingdom on earth.

The principality of Islam is the one unifying force in the diversity of the so-called Arab world. The peoples of the Middle East represent a variety of cultural and ethnic backgrounds. Some, such as the Syrians, Saudi Arabians and Iraqis are *Arabs* – descendants of **Shem**, and therefore *Semites*. Others, such as the Egyptians, Libyans and Moroccans are called Arabs, but are descendants of **Ham**. The Iranians are *Persians*, not Arabs, and harbour an historical animosity against their Arab neighbours, a fact that was tragically demonstrated in the eight year long Iran-Iraq war.

However, the common goal shared by every nation in the Moslem confederacy is the *Islamization* of the Middle East, which by implication, if not always by explicit declaration, calls for the destruction of the State of Israel. For the dismantling of the Jewish State is, above all things, a religious duty.

The Third World War

The principality of Islam is on a collision course with the Spirit of God, and the Prophetic Word indicates that the clash will ultimately take place on the mountains of Israel.

In chapters 38 and 39 of Ezekiel, the prophet describes a massive assault on Israel by a confederacy of forces headed up by *Gog, of the land of Magog, the prince of Rosh, Meshech, and Tubal.*

Also included in the coalition are *Gomer, the house of Togarmah, Persia, Cush,* and *Put.*

According to *Young's Concordance*, the land of **Magog** is located north of the Caucasus Mountains between the Black and Caspian Seas. The descendants of **Magog**, a grandson of Noah, settled in a vast area of Eastern Europe and Central Asia known as **Scythia**. The Jewish historian **Josephus** states that the descendants of **Gog** were later known as the *Scythians*, whom he says were otherwise known as *Magogites*. These people subsequently formed the greater part of *Russian* stock.

The prince of **Rosh**, or more literally, 'chief prince', signifies the inhabitants of *Scythia*. From it the *Russians* derive their name.

The people of **Meshech** and **Tubal** roamed the same area, from the Baltic Sea to the Ural Mountains. **Russia** was known as *Muskovi* until the time of Ivan the Terrible, a name undoubtedly connected with **Meshech**. It is possible that the two famous Russian cities of **Moscow** and **Tobolsk** still preserve the elements of the names **Meshech** and **Tubal**.[5]

Thus, the area referred to in the prophecy as *Magog, Rosh, Meshech, Tubal,* and *Togarmah* can be readily identified as the former **USSR**, now known as the **Commonwealth of Independent States** (CIS).

The descendants of **Gomer** moved from north of the Black Sea westward, some to the south, and others through Europe, and are identified as the *Germanic people*.

Togarmah's descendants occupied the southern part of the nation we know as **Russia**, along with **Rumania**, **Bulgaria**, **Turkey** and **Armenia**.

According to Ezekiel's prophecy, the northern confederacy will be joined by forces from the East, including **Persia** (modern-day **Iran** and **Iraq**), **Cush** (**Ethiopia**) and **Put** (**Libya**).

It is interesting to consider this tapestry of nations and territories in light of the modern geographical spread of Islam.

Moslems are in the majority in six of the fifteen former Soviet Republics: Azerbaijan, Kazakhstan, Tajikistan, Kirgizia, Uzbekistan and Turkmenistan. However, these republics are among the smallest and poorest in the Commonwealth, and are vulnerable to overtures from the oil-rich Arab/Persian world.

Indeed, fundamentalist Iran has dispatched 'missionaries' throughout the Moslem world, and in particular, the Central Asian republics, to fan the flames of Islamic revolution. Moreover, Teheran is utilizing its formidable oil assets to bankroll fundamentalist terrorist organizations such as the Lebanese based *Hizbullah*, the Palestinian *Islamic Jihad*, and more recently, *Hamas*.

Iranian guns, money and advisers are shoring up some regimes and undermining others. Its agents are feverishly at work in Cairo, Amman, Algiers, Tunis, Khartoum, eastern Saudi Arabia, Bahrain and the United Arab Emirates.

This program of destabilization is but a means to an end – namely, the Islamization of the Middle East, and eventually the world.

'The struggle against Israel is paramount' says Iran's supreme spiritual leader, **Ayatollah Ali Khameini**. And according to his powerful radical colleague, **Ayatollah Ahmad Jannati**, Iran is activating agents around the world for 'the Third World War' – between Islam and the West.

The Islamic Bomb

Since the end of the Iran-Iraq War, and particularly, the Persian Gulf War, Iran has been engaged in a massive arms build-up, which includes the purchase of Russian nuclear submarines, advanced Scud-C missiles from North Korea, and a whole array of state-of-the-art weapons from China. Recent intelligence reports indicate that Iran has already purchased a nuclear device from a former Soviet republic and is currently working on delivery systems, as well as cooperating with other countries in the Middle East and North Africa to manufacture its own long range ground-to-ground missiles.

As well as stockpiles of military hardware, there is an increasing traffic in scientific and technical personnel. The brain-drain of out-of-work Soviet nuclear scientists is considered to be more dangerous ultimately than the trade in nuclear weapons materials.

The acquisition of the Bomb has been the goal and dream of many Arab leaders. Libya's **Muammar Gadaffi** entertained the fantasy of becoming a modern **Saladin**, and financed Pakistani nuclear research in the hope that they would present him with an 'Islamic Bomb'. Furthermore, he made no secret of the fact that the intended purpose of this weapon was to obliterate Israel.

From President Gamal Abdel Nasser to Saddam Hussein,

Arab rulers have shared a common belief that the road to leadership in the Arab/Moslem world passes through the ruins of Israel. This notion is also prevalent amongst the Ayatollahs of Iran.

But history has proven that the annihilation of Israel cannot be achieved by conventional methods alone. The atomic bomb is seen therefore, as the 'final solution' to the 'Jewish problem'.

The fact that the six Islamic republics in question accommodate 20% of the former Soviet Union's nuclear power should give great cause for concern, if not prayer. And all the more so as they come under the sway of their rabid, fundamentalist neighbours in Iran.

Iran sees itself as an impending superpower in the Middle East, and has cleverly taken advantage of Saddam Hussein's Gulf War defeat to assume the mantle of leadership in the Arab/Moslem world.

There are ominous rumblings in Iran's government-controlled press. Radio and newspapers openly speak of the destruction of Israel. Since the death of Ayatollah Khomeini, the political rhetoric of Iran's ruling *mullahs* has become increasingly virulent and their denunciations of Israel have become even sharper. Indeed, the Ayatollah's successors appear to be trying to 'out-Khomeini' Khomeini!

Through the merger of Iran's religious zeal and the Central Asian republics' technological resources, Islam is positioning itself for the final stage of world conquest.

God has been speaking to many prophets and intercessors about a final confrontation with Islam on the mountains of Israel. I wish to quote from two such messages, and would ask the reader to prayerfully consider what the Spirit of God is saying:

> 'During this same period the Soviets, in league with Iran and other Islamic nations, will march against Israel with worldwide public opinion on their side. No other country will help Israel but the assault will be stopped by an earthquake and great storms. This will so undeniably be an act of God that it will also stop the assault against Christians as

well, fanning the flames of revival until believers will have to hide in order to sleep because of the multitudes seeking salvation. This will be the most glorious advance that the church is to make before the return of the Lord. The Jews and the Gentiles were meant to be one loaf (see Ephesians 2:14–18). The plan will not be complete until they are joined *in Christ*.'[6]

A similar word was delivered by Lance Lambert at a prophetic conference on Mount Carmel, in 1986.

'And hear this! Do not fear the power of the Kremlin nor the power of the Islamic Revolution, for I plan to break both of them through Israel. I will bring down their pride and their arrogance, and shatter them because they have blasphemed My Name. In that day, I will avenge the blood of all the martyrs and of the innocent ones whom they have slaughtered. I will surely do this thing, for they have thought that there was no one to judge them. But I have seen their ways and I have heard the cries of the oppressed and of the persecuted, and I will break their power and make an end of them. Be therefore prepared, for when all this comes to pass you will be given the last great opportunity to preach the Gospel freely to all the nations.'[7]

The dethroning of the principality of Islam will result in one of the greatest evangelical harvests in church history. Millions of Moslems from all over the world will come to a saving knowledge of Jesus the Messiah.

The reign of darkness, which C.S. Lewis, in his novel *The Silver Chair*, calls the 'spell of Underland', will at last be broken, and multitudes will be free to come to the light.

Rick Joyner makes the following prophetic observation:

'As the harvest begins to affect Islamic countries, some will vehemently resist it, but in general the harvest will reap many from Islam. Egypt will be entirely won to the Lord; her devotion and willingness to sacrifice for His purposes will be so great she will actually be called "the altar of the Lord". Great apostles and prophets will come out of Islamic countries. These will rejoice greatly in the truth that sets them free, preaching the Gospel with a commitment and abandon which will inspire the entire Body of Christ.'[8]

Many intercessors believe that the Gulf War signalled the first crack in the wall of Islam. Indeed, since that time there have been reports of spiritually-hungry Moslems coming to faith in the Lord Jesus in Mecca itself! As the Apostle Paul said, *'The Word of God is not bound!'* Hallelujah!

Spiritual Warfare

The real conflict in the Middle East is depicted in Psalm 83 by the prophetic singer Asaph:

> *'Do not keep silent, O God! Do not hold your peace, and do not be still, O God! For behold, Your enemies make a tumult; and those who hate You have lifted up their head.'*
> (Psalm 83:1, 2)

First of all, the Psalmist identifies the spiritual nature of the conflict. The *enemies of God* are making a tumult or an uproar; those who *hate the LORD* are exalting themselves in pride.

This revelation puts the whole conflict into proper perspective. The aggressors are primarily enemies of the Lord and His purposes, and secondarily enemies of Israel and the Church.

> *'They have taken crafty counsel against Your people, and consulted together against Your sheltered ones. They have said, "Come, and let us cut them off from being a nation, that the name of Israel may be remembered no more." For they have consulted together with one consent; they form a confederacy against You ... who said, "Let us take for ourselves the pastures of God for a possession."'*
> (Psalm 83:3–5, 12)

Satan has only once dared to mount a direct assault on the Throne of God, on which occasion he suffered a humiliating and unmitigated defeat. Lucifer, as he was then known, was banished from Heaven, together with his fellow mutineers, to the atmospheric heavens surrounding the earth.

From that point on, Satan's war against the Almighty went 'underground'. Satan knew that he could no longer attack God directly, so he did the next best thing: he attacked the creature God loved the most – Man. Hence the temptation in the Garden of Eden.

Thus, the stage was set for a war against the Lord by proxy – a guerilla campaign against God's chosen people.

Consequently, Israel finds herself at the centre of a spiritual war which is beyond her natural comprehension. Israel knows that she is surrounded by hostile nations which are bent on destroying her. But the motivation behind this irrational and unwarranted hatred is hidden from her eyes.

To facilitate her destruction, Israel's enemies take 'crafty counsel' against her. Terrorist organizations give lip service to United Nations' resolutions acknowledging Israel's right to exist, and multiple murderers are hailed as ambassadors of peace by politicians and reporters alike.

> *'Deal with them as with Midian, as with Sisera, as with Jabin at the Brook Kishon, who perished at En Dor, who became as refuse on the earth. Make their nobles like Oreb and like Zeeb, yes all their princes like Zebah and Zalmunna ... O my God, make them like the whirling dust, like the chaff before the wind! As the fire burns the woods, and as the flame sets the mountains on fire, so pursue them with Your tempest, and frighten with Your storm.*
>
> *Fill their faces with shame, that they may seek Your name, O LORD. Let them be confounded and dismayed forever; yes, let them be put to shame and perish. That men may know that You, whose name alone is the LORD, are the Most High over all the earth.'* (Psalm 83:9–11, 13–18)

Herein is the victory of the Kingdom of God over the power

of the Evil One. The Lord God, in response to the petitions of His people, will intervene with a mighty hand and an outstretched arm. He will come and save; He will arise and deliver!

God has interceded supernaturally in people's lives before, and He will do so again. He will overturn the schemes of evil men and bring their counsel to naught. He will send confusion into the camp of the enemy. His angels will disperse and pursue them seven ways. They will be driven away like chaff by the wind of God's Spirit, and scattered like dust by the whirlwind of His power.

All who resist the Lord and His people will be ashamed and dismayed, yes, even bewildered and terrified at the terror of the Lord and the glory of His majesty, when He arises to shake the earth mightily! (see Isaiah 2)

Yet, in the midst of judgment there will be redemption: people will come face to face with the sovereignty of God and the Lordship of Messiah, and will be motivated to seek the Lord with all their hearts!

For even out of 'great tribulation' God will gather a people for His Name! (Revelation 7:13–14).

References

1. *The Story of the Church*, Vol. III, p. 113. The Church of Scotland Committee on Youth (1934).
2. *The Christian Mid-East Conference*, PO Box 82, Poway, California, 92064, USA.
3. *Encounter with Hamas* by Joel Greenberg, The Jerusalem Post International Edition, March, 1990.
4. *The Iranian Revolution and the Muslim World*, by Elie Rekhess, Westview Press, 1990.
5. *Noah's Three Sons* by Arthur Custance, Zondervan. Pt II, Ch. 2: 'The Family of Japheth'.
6. *The Harvest*, by Rick Joyner. Morningstar Publications, Pineville, NC, p. 139.
7. *He will tell you things to come*. Derek Prince Ministries, PO Box 300, Fort Lauderdale, Florida, 33302, USA.
8. *The Harvest*, by Rick Joyner. Morningstar Publications, Pineville, NC, pp. 128–129.

Chapter 11

Seizing the Kingdom by Intrigue

'And in his place shall arise a vile person, to whom they will not give the honor of royalty; but he shall come in peaceably, and seize the kingdom by intrigue. With the force of a flood they shall be swept away from before him and be broken, and also the prince of the covenant. And after the league is made with him he shall act deceitfully, for he shall come up and become strong with a small number of people.'
(Daniel 11:21–23)

On Monday, September 13th, 1993, the world watched in amazement as PLO Chairman Yasser Arafat, avowed enemy of the Jewish people and self-proclaimed liberator of Jerusalem, shook hands with Israeli Prime Minister Yitzhak Rabin, a veteran of the élite *Palmach* force and IDF Chief of Staff during the 1967 Six Day War.

Waves of euphoria swept the globe as the international community contemplated the prospect of 'peace in our time'. The dissenting voices of genuinely concerned Israelis and radical Islamic fundamentalists were drowned in a chorus of media-inspired approval.

Handshakes, smiles, and letters of mutual recognition notwithstanding, serious questions remain to be answered with regard to the 'Gaza-Jericho First' proposal, and indeed, the whole concept of Palestinian-Arab autonomy in the territories.

The sincerity of Yasser Arafat's commitment to recognize Israel's right to exist in peace and security is highly questionable, considering his statement on September 1st, 1993, that 'this is the

Phases Plan that we accepted in 1974' – a plan that calls for the liberation of Palestine in stages; obtaining whatever possible by peaceful means, in preparation for a final military assault by the Arab regimes, once Israel is dwarfed and weakened – a statement that he repeated on Jordanian television just hours after the signing of the Declaration of Principles on the White House lawn!

Moreover, the veracity of the PLO's commitment to a peaceful resolution of the Israeli-Palestinian Arab conflict, and its renunciation of terrorism and violence is extremely doubtful in view of the disunity within the PLO executive committee (only nine of the committee's eighteen members approved the agreement to recognize Israel, with two having resigned and three others abstaining along with 'Foreign Minister' Farouk Kaddoumi).

The mainstream faction of the PLO, *Fatah*, to which Arafat belongs, has been responsible for the murder of hundreds of 'collaborators' in the territories since the start of the Intifada in December, 1987, surpassing radical fundamentalist groups like *Hamas* in acts of violence and terror. One wonders how a gang of murderers, rapists and robbers will be transformed into a law-abiding 'Palestinian Police Force' that protects human rights and upholds democratic freedoms!

For this reason, my sympathy lies with the average Palestinian man-in-the-street, who, in the final analysis, will be the victim of this 'peace plan'. If a PLO State does emerge west of the Jordan, there is no doubt but that it will be a police-state in the very best traditions of brutal totalitarianism.

Furthermore, the potential in such a State or even such an autonomous region for internecine warfare is enormous. Fundamentalist groups like *Hamas* and *Islamic Jihad* refuse to recognize Israel's right to exist and entertain no thought of negotiation with the Zionist enemy. In some parts of the territories, these movements command a significant following, if not a majority of popular support.

With death threats being issued against Arafat's life, and denouncements being made concerning the PLO's capitulation to Israeli demands, the stage is set for a vicious and bloody confrontation to determine who will have the honour of representing Islam in the battle for '*El Quds*' (the holy city) and the Land west of the Jordan.

The Trojan Horse of Palestine

A PLO State in Judea and Samaria (commonly known as the 'West Bank') would be nothing less than a Trojan Horse in the very heartland of *Eretz* Israel – the perfect beachhead from which to launch terrorist attacks against population centres in the north, the centre and the south of the Jewish nation. Whereas the Israel Defence Force and the General Security Service previously had the power to pursue and apprehend terrorists anywhere in the Territories, under the 'Gaza-Jericho First Plan' (stage one), and the 'West Bank Autonomy Plan' (stage two), they would have to rely on the cooperation of the 'Palestinian Police Force' to arrest terrorists who had successfully returned to their homes and bases in PLO controlled areas.

Thus, if the 'Peace Plan' is but another stage in the 'Phased Plan for the liberation of the whole of Palestine' as Yasser Arafat has stated, it is quite conceivable that the 'Palestinian Police Force' would be instructed to 'protect' terrorists who managed to slip back into the territories after completing their missions of murder and destruction in Israel proper.

Indeed, some of Israel's leading defence experts have expressed serious doubts about the possibility of cooperating with the 'Palestinian Police' in the war against terrorism. In an address to the Knesset Foreign Affairs and Defense Committee, Deputy Chief of General Staff Major-General Amnon Shahak, said: 'It will be extremely difficult to conduct preventive action against terrorism, and it will be extremely difficult to eradicate terrorism without preventive action.' Moreover, Shahak said that he did not know how the security forces would protect Israelis travelling on roads inside the autonomous Palestinian areas, or how they would continue to apprehend wanted Palestinian suspects. He also warned that the security forces would not be able to continue their activities against wanted Palestinian suspects if they would have to coordinate their moves with the Palestinian police force.[1]

Shlomo Gazit, former head of military intelligence and former coordinator of government activities in the territories, said that a strong Palestinian police force would be insufficient to prevent terrorist attacks from Gaza. But incredibly, he then added, 'An agreement is tested by the ability of both sides to maintain it. If, for instance, the Palestinians are unable to enforce the halt to terrorist attacks, then the worst case would be Israel tearing up the paper.'[2]

Incredible, because any astute observer should know that once Yasser Arafat and the PLO are entrenched in the territories, they will sooner or later proclaim a Palestinian State. Significantly, the agreement between Israel and the PLO does not call on the PLO to renounce its 1988 declaration of Statehood, or to make any change in its worldwide network of embassies. Thus, the rapid evolution of an autonomous administration in Gaza-Jericho to statehood is practically inevitable, with the PLO seeking to expand its jurisdiction throughout Judea and Samaria (the West Bank). That such a State will be recognized by most of the world is a given. And as David Bar-Illan, Executive Editor of the *Jerusalem Post* wrote,

> 'If the minuscule Palestinian State then becomes what the PLO ministate in Lebanon was in the late 1970s and early 1980s – a springboard for terrorist activities against Israel – it will be virtually impossible to act effectively against it. Those who believe that if the experiment does not work, the Israeli army can invade the districts and restore the *status quo ante*, are obviously unaware of the world's attitude. It is one thing to carve out a narrow security zone in an unstable neighbouring country, and quite another to eradicate a recognized sovereignty.'[3]

Any interference by Israel in the sovereign affairs of 'Palestine', whether it be to root out terrorist cells or to ensure the security of Jewish settlers, or any protracted intransigence on the part of Israel's leaders with respect to the status of East

Jerusalem, 'the capital of Palestine,' could be seized upon by surrounding Arab nations as a pretext for war.

And in the case of war, PLO mortars and artillery, and even missiles, could be stationed less than forty miles from Tel Aviv, and less than ten miles from Jewish Jerusalem!

A Treacherous Peace

Sadly, the gullibility of some of Israel's leaders is a wonder to behold. I cannot help but feel that it is somehow connected with the original rejection of the Messiah. To the unbelieving religious leaders, Jesus said, *'I have come in My Father's name, and you do not receive Me; if another comes in his own name, him you will receive'* (John 5:43).

However, God is always faithful to warn His people of impending deception. The prophet Daniel received a revelation from God concerning the plan of redemption and the destiny of Israel whilst in exile in Babylon during the Sixth Century BC. He was also given understanding of the 'times of the Gentiles' – the successive cycles of Gentile political authority, culminating in the Second Advent of Messiah and the judgment of the nations.

The prophecy is interspersed with warnings concerning a king who would *'come in peaceably and seize the kingdom by intrigue,'* and later *'act deceitfully'* and *'return in rage against the holy covenant and do damage.'*

> *'...therefore he shall be grieved, and return in rage against the holy covenant, and do damage. So he shall return and show regard for those who forsake the holy covenant. And forces shall be mustered by him, and they shall defile the sanctuary fortress; then they shall take away the daily sacrifices, and place there the abomination of desolation. Those who do wickedly against the covenant he shall corrupt with flattery; but the people who know their God shall be strong, and carry out great exploits. And those of the people who understand shall instruct many; yet for many days they shall fall by sword and flame, by captivity and plundering. Now*

> *when they fall, they shall be aided with a little help; but*
> *many shall join with them by intrigue. And some of those of*
> *understanding shall fall, to refine them, purify them, and*
> *make them white, until the time of the end; because it is still*
> *for the appointed time.'* (Daniel 11:29–35)

This prophecy was fulfilled to the letter by Antiochus IV, the Seleucid king who ruled from 175 BC to 164 BC. Called **Epiphanes** (illustrious), but nicknamed **Epimanes** (madman) by his enemies, Antiochus distinguished himself as the most ferocious persecutor of the Jewish nation in the Old Testament era, so much so, that the prophecy of Daniel depicts him as the archetypal antichrist.

Secular historians describe Antiochus as an odd-humoured man, rude and boisterous, base and sordid. He had nothing in him of princely qualities, and had for some time been a hostage and prisoner at Rome, from whence he made his escape. By a trick he got his elder brother's son, Demetrius, to be sent to Rome in a kind of hostage exchange, and following the assassination of his brother, Seleucus, he took the kingdom.

Antiochus would sometimes steal out of the court into the city, and associate with infamous company *incognito*; carefully disguised, he made himself a companion of the common sort, and of the basest strangers that came to town. He had the most unaccountable whims, so that some took him to be silly, others to be mad.

However, Antiochus was also a fervent believer in Hellenic (Greek) culture and civilization, and possessed an extraordinary love of art. He was a man of great ingenuity, and a master of dissimulation and deceit. His vision was to unite the nations of the Eastern Mediterranean basin in a pan-Hellenic 'common market' – a revived Alexandrian empire. Under the pretence of treaties, leagues, and alliances, Antiochus encroached on people's sovereign rights, and tricked them into subjection. The keynote of his policy was 'unity', and to this end, he sought to impose Greek culture, thought and customs on the nations under his dominion, and to eradicate 'parochialism', whether in culture, language or religion.

Interestingly enough, a 'progressive party' emerged in Israel at about the same time which sought to throw off the shackles of 'medieval religion' and help the nation take its place in the rapidly developing 'New World Order'.

It was then that there emerged from Israel a set of renegades who led many people astray. *'"Come," they said, "let us reach an understanding with the pagans surrounding us, for since we separated ourselves from them many misfortunes have overtaken us." This proposal proved acceptable, and a number of the people eagerly approached the king, who authorized them to practise the pagan observances'* (1 Maccabees 1:12–14, Jerusalem Bible).

Antiochus supported the Hellenizer, Jason, in his bid to become the Jewish High Priest, who promptly set about establishing a school at Jerusalem for the training up of the youth in the fashions of the heathen, and enrolling men as Antiochists, a company which organized athletic interests and festivities.

Under the influence of Jason and other perfidious apostate Jewish leaders, Grecian customs were introduced, theatres and gymnasiums were built, and all religions were regarded as alike. People continued to sacrifice to Yahweh, but at the same time sent money for sacrifices to Hercules. In the words of the Second Book of Maccabees, *'They disdained all that their ancestors had esteemed, and set the highest value on hellenic honours. But all this brought its own retribution; the very people whose way of life they envied, whom they sought to resemble in everything, proved to be their enemies and executioners'* (2 Maccabees 4:15–16, Jerusalem Bible).

When Antiochus visited Jerusalem, he was given a magnificent welcome by Jason and the city, and was received with torches and acclamations. But Antiochus was obsessed with the design of reducing the Jews to a conformity of manners and religion with other nations; or, in other words, of abolishing those distinctive features which made the Jews a peculiar people, socially separated from all others. This design was odious to the great body of the people, although there were many among the higher classes who regarded it with favour.

Of this way of thinking was Menelaus, whom Antiochus had

made High Priest in the place of Jason, and who was expelled by the orthodox Jews with ignominy in 169 BC, when they heard the joyful news that Antiochus had been slain in Egypt. The rumour proved untrue, and Antiochus on his return punished them by plundering and profaning the temple. Guided by Menelaus, he entered the sanctuary with blasphemies, and took away the gold and silver vessels, an action that provoked deep mourning throughout Israel.

But worse evils were to befall them two years later, in 167 BC Antiochus, infuriated because he could not gain his point in Egypt by reason of the Romans interposing, wreaked his revenge upon the poor Jews, who gave him no provocation, but had greatly provoked God to permit him to do it. He sent his chief collector of tribute, Apollonius, with a detachment of 22,000 men, to destroy Jerusalem. Addressing the people with what appeared to be peaceful words, Apollonius gained their confidence, and then suddenly fell on the city, dealing it a terrible blow. He pillaged the city and set it on fire, tore down its houses and encircling wall, took the women and children captive and put thousands of people to the sword. Using the stones of the wall, Apollonius built a citadel commanding the temple mount, from whence his soldiers fell on and slew the worshippers, so that the temple service was discontinued.

The peculiar observances of the Jewish law such as Circumcision, Sabbath-rest, and Bible reading were prohibited; immoral rites were performed in the sanctuary, and promoted throughout the land; faithful Jews were forced to eat non-kosher food, especially pork; inspectors were appointed to enforce the king's policies in all the cities of Judah; Books of the Law were torn up and burned; anyone found to be possessing a copy of the Covenant or practising the Law was sentenced to death; and a violent persecution was commenced against all who adhered to the 'old ways' and refused to sacrifice to idols.

On December 8th, 167 BC, Antiochus erected the abomination of desolation in the temple – a statue of Olympian Zeus – and at its dedication, sprinkled the blood of a pig in the Holy of Holies.

During the next three years (167 to 164 BC), it was almost

impossible to stay alive and remain uncompromised. Jerusalem was deserted by priests and people, and the daily sacrifice at the altar was entirely discontinued, being replaced by the daily sacrifice of a pig.

The enemies of the Covenant People took advantage of the Sabbath to slay them on the day when they would not fight. Some were roasted alive in caves where they had retired to keep the Sabbath; women were put to death for having their children circumcised, and their infants were hanged about their necks; and the land fairly ran with the blood of the faithful.

Antiochus went near to extirpating the worship of Yahweh. But, as Matthew Henry points out in his commentary, God would not have permitted it if His people had not provoked Him to do so. It was 'by reason of transgression', to correct them, that Antiochus was employed to give them all this trouble. Thus, he was *Flagellum Dei*, the rod of God's chastisement.

> *'Then the king shall do according to his own will: he shall exalt and magnify himself above every god, shall speak blasphemies against the God of gods, and shall prosper till the wrath has been accomplished; for what has been determined shall be done. He shall regard neither the God of his fathers nor the desire of women, nor regard any god; for he shall exalt himself above them all. But in their place he shall honour a god of fortresses; and a god which his fathers did not know he shall honour with gold and silver, with precious stones and pleasant things. Thus he shall act against the strongest fortresses with a foreign god, which he shall acknowledge, and advance its glory; and he shall cause them to rule over many, and divide the land for gain ... And he shall plant the tents of his palace between the seas and the glorious holy mountain; yet he shall come to his end, and no one will help him.'* (Daniel 11:36–39, 45)

This led to the celebrated revolt of the Maccabees, (commemorated in the Festival of *Hannukah*), who, after an arduous and sanguinary struggle, obtained possession of Jerusalem in 163 BC. They repaired and purified the temple, which was then dilapidated and deserted; provided new utensils for the sacred services; took away the old altar which had been polluted by heathen sacrifices, and erected a new one in its place; and finally, recommenced the sacrifices, exactly three years after the temple had been dedicated to Olympian Zeus.

And what of Antiochus? Hearing that the Jews had cast the image of Olympian Zeus out of the temple where he had placed it, he was so enraged that he vowed to make Jerusalem a common burial ground, and determined to march there immediately. But no sooner had he spoken these proud words than he was struck with an incurable plague in his bowels; worms bred so fast in his body that whole flakes of flesh sometimes dropped from him. His torments were violent, and the stench of his disease such that none could bear to come near him.

At first he persisted in his threats against the Jews, but at length, despairing of his recovery, he called his friends together and acknowledged that all these miseries had fallen upon him for the injuries he had done to the Jews and his profaning of the temple at Jerusalem. Then he wrote courteous letters to the Jews and vowed that if he recovered he would let them exercise their religion in freedom. But, finding his condition worsening, and when he could no longer endure his own smell, he said, 'It is meet to submit to God, and for man who is mortal not to set himself in competition with God,' and so died miserably in a strange land, on the mountains of Pacata near Babylon, about 160 years before the birth of Jesus the Messiah.

A New Kind of Hellenism

Speaking to His disciples just days before His crucifixion, the Lord Jesus addressed the all-important subject of the end of the age.

> *'"Therefore when you see the 'abomination of desolation,' spoken of by Daniel the prophet, standing in the holy place" (whoever reads, let him understand), "then let those who are in Judea flee to the mountains . . . for then there will be great*

> *tribulation, such as has not been since the beginning of the world until this time, no, nor ever shall be. And unless those days were shortened, no flesh would be saved; but for the elect's sake those days will be shortened."'*
>
> (Matthew 24:15–16, 21–22)

This prophecy of the Lord Jesus bears immediate reference to the besiegement of Jerusalem and the destruction of the temple by the Roman Legion in AD 70. However, the language and the context would indicate a further and ultimate fulfilment at the end of the age.

For example, Jesus describes it as a period of *'great tribulation, the like of which has not occurred from the beginning of the world down to the present time, nor ever will again.'* As bad as the siege of Jerusalem was, it couldn't possibly be construed as the greatest time of tribulation in the history of the world!

Furthermore, Jesus stated that *'immediately after the tribulation of those days the sun will be darkened, and the moon will not give its light; the stars will fall from heaven, and the powers of the heaven will be shaken,'* something which obviously did not occur in AD 70!

The great tribulation and the shaking of the heavens and the earth are apocalyptic events, singularly associated with the end of the age and the return of the Lord. There remains to be revealed another 'Antiochus' – the final Antichrist – who, like his predecessor, will raise up the 'abomination of desolation' in the place of Divine worship. Thus, one can safely conclude that the coming of this Lawless One will be accompanied by a 'New Hellenism' – an international order of finance, government, culture and religion – in the spirit and tradition of Antiochus Epiphanes.

As I understand it, the same 'Hellenizing forces' that were at work in Israel in the Second Century BC, are alive and well today, and are primarily responsible for negotiating the peace agreement with the PLO. For these modern Hellenizers, some of whom are serving in Government and high public office, this agreement is but the first step in a comprehensive acquiescence to the New World Order – an acquiescence that will see the

nation of Israel sacrificing its distinctive Jewish character upon
the altar of international respectability.

Stan Goodenough, Editor of the *Middle East Intelligence
Digest*, published by the International Christian Embassy
Jerusalem, recently observed that

> 'Now, just 44 years after returning as a nation to its land,
> present-day Israel finds itself in an almost identical world
> environment to the one endured under Antiochus III (Epi-
> phanes' father), 2,000 years ago. A dominant world power,
> its policies shaped by growing international political and
> economic upheaval, is exerting its influence across the
> globe. External pressure to conform to this man-centred
> world order conflicts with the Jewish nation's interests and
> increasingly erodes its sovereignty. Nonetheless its seems
> that this time Israel's leaders are mounting less of a strug-
> gle to resist. And who knows when a modern-day Epi-
> phanes might show?
>
> Paradoxically then, after centuries of keeping the faith
> and resisting conformity abroad, Israel is now being swept
> up in the race towards international acceptance and
> ultimately to assimilation in the Global Village. "We dare
> not hesitate, for the world will not wait for the Middle
> East," said Foreign Minister Shimon Peres before the UN
> General Assembly on October 1st, as he attempted to urge
> the peace process forward. It is Peres' deepest concern –
> shared by most members of the new Israeli government –
> that Israel must either march to the beat of the new world
> order or risk being left behind...'[4]

> 'Many Israelis will from the outset want to comply with UN
> demands out of fear of either annoying the world, or of
> losing trade and other privileges. Under Israel's new gov-
> ernment especially, a great effort will be made to be "in
> with the world", to be accommodating, and to integrate
> into the new world order ... This hellenization of Israel,
> bringing her in line with the wishes of the world, is pro-
> ceeding hand in hand with a tremendous spread of new age

philosophy and its accompanying new morality. Its out-working can be seen in the increased perception by Israelis, that they are primarily and preeminently secular people constrained to be loyal citizens of this world – this "global village" – rather than first and foremost faithful to their Jewish identity.

Thus the battle of the individual Jew in the diaspora is being repeated in Israel, where the Israeli Jew is still confronted with the same choice – whether to accommodate the Gentiles and subscribe to many of their wishes, or whether to live proudly as Jews, believing in the distinctiveness of that calling. The pressures on Israel and its leadership to conform to this new world order and new age ideology is growing tremendously. The question looms large and ominous: Will the Israeli Jew in the end, after suffering for nearly 2,000 years for his Jewish identity, now that he is finally free to express it, exchange it for one of assimilation as a good member of the family of nations, thus forfeiting the Jewish identity which was intended to make Israel unique and a light unto the nations?'[5]

The Refining Grace of Persecution

That Israel will survive, there is no doubt. But at what cost, remains to be seen. The Bible speaks of the refining fires of persecution through which God, on occasions, allows His people to pass, *'that the genuineness of your faith, being much more precious than gold that perishes, though it is tested by fire, may be found to praise, honor, and glory at the revelation of Jesus Christ'* (1 Peter 1:7).

It is this 'genuine faith' that the Lord is looking for in Israel, and if necessary, He will sit as a gold-smith and stoke up the fire of internal pressure and external persecution, and subject His ancient covenant people to the heat, until the impurities of worldliness rise to the surface and are skimmed off (Malachi 3:2–3).

Will history repeat itself? Commenting on the apparent connection between the persecution of Antiochus Epiphanes and the renaissance of Judaism prior to the advent of Messiah, the *Cyclopaedia of Biblical Literature* astutely notes,

> 'The change of policy, from conciliation to cruel persecution, which makes the reign of Epiphanes an era in the relation of the Jews to Syrian monarchy, has perhaps had great permanent moral results. It is not impossible that perseverance in the conciliating plan might have sapped the energy of Jewish national faith: While it is certain that persecution kindled their zeal and cemented their unity. Jerusalem, by its sufferings, became only the more sacred in the eyes of its absent citizens, who vied in replacing the wealth which the sacrilegious Epiphanes had ravished.'[6]

Amen! May the Lord, who is the same yesterday, today and forever, yet once more deliver Israel out of all her troubles, and make ready a people prepared for the coming of Messiah!

References

1. *The Jerusalem Post International Edition*, September 11th, 1993.
2. *The Jerusalem Post International Edition*, September 11th, 1993.
3. *The Jerusalem Post International Edition*, September 4th, 1993.
4. *The Middle East Intelligence Digest*, October 5th, 1992, PO Box 1192, Jerusalem 91010, Israel.
5. *The Middle East Intelligence Digest*, August 16th, 1992, PO Box 1192, Jerusalem 91010, Israel.
6. *The Cyclopaedia of Biblical Literature*, Volume 1, p. 170, Adam and Charles Black, Edinburgh, 1845.

Chapter 12

For Zion's Sake

'For Zion's sake I will not hold my peace, and for Jerusalem's sake I will not rest, until her righteousness goes forth as brightness, and her salvation as a lamp that burns.'
(Isaiah 62:1)

The Church is intended of God to be an instrument of blessing, not just to the reborn nation of Israel, but to the entire Jewish Diaspora.

The Apostle Paul set forth this timeless purpose of God in his letter to the believers in Rome:

'I say then, have they stumbled that they should fall? Certainly not! But through their fall, to provoke them to jealousy, salvation has come to the Gentiles ... I magnify my ministry, if by any means I may provoke to jealousy those who are my flesh and save some of them ... these also have now been disobedient, that through the mercy shown you they also may obtain mercy.' (Romans 11:11, 13, 14, 31)

In other words, God intends to restore Israel to her spiritual inheritance through the sensitive and compassionate ministry of Christian believers. Accordingly, many Christians, upon receiving a vision of God's purpose for Israel, have given of their love, time, prayers and finance to expedite the fulfilment of God's Word.

For some, the decision to identify with God's purpose in

Israel was made at great personal cost. Francis Kett, a Fellow of Corpus Christi College, Cambridge, and the first Christian in modern times to expound the biblical return of the Jews to their homeland, was burned as a heretic in 1589!

What began with individual believers must now become the responsibility of the whole Church. It is time for Christians to rise up as a united body and 'comfort Zion'.

During the decade of the 1980s the Spirit of God brought to Christians around the world a fresh awareness of their indebtedness to Israel. Together with this awareness came a new sense of responsibility to the Jewish people. The opening verses of Isaiah chapter forty became the focus of this movement of God: '"*Comfort, yes, comfort My people!*" *says your God.* "*Speak comfort to Jerusalem…*"'

The burden of the Lord for Israel cannot and must not be feigned. Rather, it must be **formed** by the Spirit of God through prayer, fasting and waiting on God.

The Bible reveals at least four ways in which we can 'comfort Zion' and discharge the burden of the Lord: *prayer*, *praise*, *prophetic proclamation* and *practical service*.

Prayer

'*My house shall be called a house of prayer*' said Jesus (Matthew 21:13). Prayer is 'the main business of the Church,' and accordingly, should take preeminence in our daily lives.

The importance of prayer with respect to God's purposes for Israel cannot be exaggerated. John Wesley once said, 'God will do nothing but in answer to prayer.' Another great pray-er, S.D. Gordon, declared, 'The greatest thing anyone can do for God and for man is to pray … you can do more than pray *after* you have prayed, but you cannot do more than pray *until* you have prayed.'

The fulfilment of God's Word concerning Israel is, to a large extent, contingent on the prayers of the Church. Prayer is indeed, the key to the future of the Jewish people.

Every movement of God's Spirit in Jewish and Christian history has been built upon the foundation of intercessory prayer. The end-time outpouring of the Spirit upon the house of David and the inhabitants of Jerusalem will be no different.

First Things First

A Christian's first responsibility toward Israel is to pray – for the manifestation of God's rule and the fulfilment of His will, 'on earth, in the Jewish nation, as it is in heaven.'

The will of God for Israel is clearly defined in His Word: *'that they may be saved'* (Romans 10:1).

The Greek words *'sozo'* (save) and *'soteria'* (salvation) represent the whole spectrum of redemption and restoration: cleansing from sin, deliverance from spiritual death, rightstanding with God, holiness (conformity to Messiah in character and conduct), mental wholeness, emotional stability, physical healing, rescue from danger and destruction, preservation from evil, safety, soundness etc.

Therefore, in praying for Israel to be saved, we are praying for the fulfilment of God's total purpose: for the veil to be removed from the Jews' spiritual eyes, that they may come to know Jesus the Messiah; for the exiles to return from the four corners of the earth and build up Zion; for the protection of the people and the security of the Land; for racial harmony and social integration; for agricultural and technological productivity and economic prosperity etc.

In the same vein, we are instructed to *'pray for the peace of Jerusalem'* (Psalm 122:6). The Hebrew word *'shalom'*, translated 'peace', denotes much more than cessation of hostilities. Like *'sozo'* and *'soteria'*, it signifies wholeness in every part of life – spiritual well-being, mental wholeness and emotional stability, physical health, economic and material prosperity, and social harmony.

The Word of God has an answer for every situation and circumstance of life. The promises of God are 'yes' and 'amen' in Messiah, to the glory of God, ***through us!*** (2 Corinthians 1:20). It is incumbent on Christian believers to take the promises of spiritual outpourings, Divine blessings, and supernatural deliverances to the Lord in prayer, and claim them in faith on behalf of Israel!

There are many things we can do and many things we should do to bless Israel, but the first thing we need to do is ***pray!***

The Apostle Paul had his priorities right when he wrote to his son-in-the-faith Timothy:

> *'Therefore I exhort **first of all** that supplications, prayers, intercessions, and giving of thanks be made for all men. For kings and all who are in authority, that we may lead a quiet and peaceable life in all godliness and reverence. For this is good and acceptable in the sight of God our Saviour, Who desires all men to be saved and to come to the knowledge of the truth ... Therefore I desire that the men pray everywhere, lifting up holy hands, without wrath and doubting.'*
> (1 Timothy 2:1–4, 8)

Praying comes before preaching, teaching or serving. Our works and our words must be birthed in prayer and bathed in prayer. Only then will they bear lasting fruit to the glory of God!

The Highest Calling

The ministry of worship and intercession is the highest calling available to man. And there is no greater assignment in intercession than to stand on behalf of God's purposes for Israel!

> *'I have set watchmen on your walls, O Jerusalem, who shall never hold their peace day or night. You who make mention of the LORD, do not keep silent, and give Him no rest till He establishes and till He makes Jerusalem a praise in the earth.'*
> (Isaiah 62:6–7)

The word 'set' indicates a Divine enlistment of prayer warriors whose special focus is the fulfilment of God's purposes in Israel. Their responsibility is to *'make mention of the Lord'* – that is, to put the Lord in remembrance of His Word and give Him no rest until He brings it to pass.

Please note that the ministry of a Watchman is by Divine

invitation and appointment. *'I have set watchmen...'* No one takes this honour to himself. It is a privilege of grace to obey the call of the Spirit.

Prayer is partnership with God in the redemption of Israel. Prayer is spiritual warfare against the powers of darkness that seek to destroy God's people and thwart God's purposes.

If we respond to the call of the Spirit and enter into the ministry of intercession we will find ourselves engaged in constant, and at times intense, spiritual warfare. This will require dedication, perseverance, and a certain spiritual 'toughness' on our part, if we are to last the distance.

God is looking for a people who will not faint in the heat of the battle or grow discouraged at the constant onslaught of the enemy, but having put on the whole armour of God, continue to cry out to Him day and night in the assurance of victory. Through warriors like this, the Kingdom of Heaven is established on earth!

A Prayer Tunnel

The importance of sustained intercession was impressed upon me recently, during a 'Shalom Israel' seminar in Melbourne. After completing the second teaching session, I felt a strong urge to call the people to prayer. As we sought the Lord together, the Spirit of Revelation came upon me and I began to prophesy. The gist of the message was as follows:

'When Jerusalem was threatened with invasion and famine by the Assyrian host, Hezekiah, King of Judah, constructed a tunnel to bring water into the city. Diggers began at both ends and worked toward the centre, tunnelling through 1770 feet of solid rock. While there were yet three cubits to excavate, the voice of one digger was heard calling to another through a crevice in the rock. Animated by the prospect of imminent success, they completed the boring through and struck pick against pick as the waters flowed freely from the spring to the pool. In like manner, God is building a "tunnel of prayer" through the religious wall that encircles Israel. Intercessors are concentrating prayer from within and without. By God's grace, they will break through the barrier of antichrist and meet in the centre, thereby cutting a path for the river of God's Spirit to flow freely into His Land and City.'

The Word of the Lord went on to call for persevering, faith-filled prayer with an assurance of ultimate breakthrough, provided we do not grow weary and give up.

Psalm of the Watchman

A watchman is one who keeps vigil, often on a tower or wall, and usually at night. At the first sight or sound of danger he is required to blow the trumpet and raise the alarm. Thus, the security of the city is dependent on his faithfulness and alertness.

The Lord is our Great Watchman, and Psalm 121 is a celebration of His great watchcare.

The Lord is ever vigilant – *'He who keeps you will not slumber. Behold, He who keeps Israel shall neither slumber nor sleep.'*

The Lord covers and protects us; He anticipates the enemy's forays and stands to our defense – *'The LORD is your keeper; the LORD is your shade at your right hand. The sun shall not strike you by day, nor the moon by night.'*

The Lord strengthens and upholds us – *'My help comes from the LORD, Who made heaven and earth. He will not allow your foot to be moved; the LORD shall preserve you from all evil; He shall preserve your soul.'*

The Lord has entered into a perpetual 'covenant of watching' – *'The LORD shall preserve your going out and your coming in from this time forth, and even for evermore.'*

The Lord is asking us, as spiritual watchmen, to make the same commitment to Jerusalem as He has made to us. We are to watch and pray, without ceasing. We are to keep our hearts with all diligence, so as not to become ensnared with the cares of this world, the deceitfulness of riches, and the desire for other things. We are to live simply, so as to devote ourselves to the God-appointed ministry of intercession.

We are to protect and defend God's purpose in Jerusalem. Through the Spirit of wisdom and revelation and the power of intercessory prayer, we are to anticipate the enemy's schemes and purchase a season of restraint for the people of God. By God's grace we are to enter into a 'covenant of watching' – a life-long commitment to God's purpose and God's city!

A watchman, spiritually speaking, is a prophet and an intercessor – one who *sees* the Lord's vision, *hears* the Lord's Word, and *proclaims* the Lord's message (Ezekiel 33:1–9).

May God's watchmen raise their voices and shout together in triumph, as they see with their own eyes the Lord returning to Zion! Hallelujah!

Praise

Throughout the Bible God's people are instructed to sing and rejoice because of the redemption of Zion.

> *'Surely these shall come from afar; Look! Those from the north and the west, and these from the land of Sinim. Sing, O heavens! Be joyful, O earth! And break out in singing, O mountains! For the LORD has comforted His people, and will have mercy on His afflicted.'* (Isaiah 49:12–13)

Furthermore,

> *'Your watchmen shall lift up their voices, with their voices they shall sing together; for they shall see eye to eye when the LORD brings back Zion. Break forth into joy, sing together; your waste places of Jerusalem! For the LORD has comforted His people, He has redeemed Jerusalem.'* (Isaiah 52:8–9)

And finally,

> *'For thus says the LORD: "Sing with gladness for Jacob, and shout among the chief of the nations; proclaim, give praise, and say, 'O LORD, save Your people, the remnant of Israel!'*

> *Behold, I will bring them from the north country, and gather them from the ends of the earth...'''*
>
> (Jeremiah 31:7–8)

Praise is one of the most powerful spiritual weapons available to man. The Psalmist declared: *'You are holy, Who inhabit the praises of Israel'* (Psalm 22:3). The Hebrew word *'yashav'*, translated 'inhabit', contains the idea of 'enthronement' – to sit as a king or a judge.

God is the Great King over all the earth. His Kingdom power is manifested wherever and whenever two or three gather in His Name to praise Him with all their hearts!

In Second Chronicles chapter twenty, God 'inhabited' the praises of Jehoshaphat's choir, and set ambushes against the invading forces of Ammon, Moab, and Mount Seir, and as a result, they killed and destroyed one another!

In Acts chapter sixteen, God 'inhabited' the praises of Paul and Silas as they languished in the Philippian jail. A great earthquake shook the foundation of the prison, opened all the doors and loosed everyone's chains, and resulted in the salvation of the warden and his household!

Furthermore, praise paralyses the enemy and silences his accusations. Psalm 8:2 says, *'Out of the mouth of babes and infants You have ordained strength, because of Your enemies, that You may silence the enemy and the avenger.'*

When Jesus quoted this passage of Scripture upon entering the Temple, He substituted the word *praise* for the word *strength*. Praise to God in the mouth of babes and infants becomes spiritual strength in the hand of the Lord which silences the voice of the Evil One!

The potency of praise is portrayed in Psalm 149. The first five verses describe various expressions of praise to God: singing, rejoicing, dancing, music. The next four verses highlight the tremendous power that is unleashed through praise, and the devastating effect it has upon the enemy:

> *'Let the high praises of God be in their mouth, and a two-edged sword in their hand, to execute vengeance on the*

nations, and punishments on the peoples; To bind their kings with chains, and their nobles with fetters of iron; to execute on them the written judgment – this honour have all His saints. Praise the LORD!'

Our primary conflict is not with human beings. The 'kings and nobles' with which we contend are spiritual entities enthroned in heavenly places (Ephesians 6:12). But God has placed in our hands weapons that are mighty in Messiah Jesus for pulling down strongholds of Satan, and casting down arguments and every high thing that exalts itself against the knowledge of God! (2 Corinthians 10:4–5)

Rise up saints of God to this your honour! Take up the sword of the Spirit and sing aloud the praises of the Lord! For the Lord has given us this day to rejoice and to triumph in His praise!

Prophetic Proclamation

The 'prophetic' or anointed proclamation of God's Word is another powerful spiritual weapon in the arsenal of the Church of Messiah Jesus.

The legal basis of our victory over Satan is the 'Blood of the Lamb' – the death, burial and resurrection of Jesus. However, the victory and authority of the Cross must be expressed and applied through the 'Word of our Testimony' (Revelation 12:11).

There is a special ministry of proclamation associated with the regathering of the Jewish people and the rebirth of the nation of Israel:

'For thus says the LORD: "Sing with gladness for Jacob, and shout among the chief of the nations; proclaim, give praise, and say, 'O LORD, save Your people, the remnant of Israel!' Hear the Word of the LORD, O nations, and declare it in the isles afar off, and say, 'He who scattered Israel will gather him, and keep him as a shepherd does his flock.'"'

(Jeremiah 31:7, 10)

As Christians, we are charged with the responsibility of proclaiming the good news of God's Rule to all people and all nations. An essential part of God's Kingdom purpose, and therefore of our message, is the regathering and restoration of Israel.

The truth about Israel must be shouted among the nations and declared in the isles afar off. God is raising up a prophetic Church that will prophesy to many peoples, nations, tongues and kings (Revelation 10:11).

Our message to the world is two-fold:

Firstly, the regathering and restoration of Israel is an act of God, a fulfilment of His Word, and an expression of His sovereignty.

Secondly, God is committed to Israel's future and He has taken personal responsibility for her protection and preservation.

May it be said of this generation of believers: *'The Lord gave the Word; great was the company of those who proclaimed it'* (Psalm 68:11).

Practical Service

In the final analysis, the call to 'comfort Zion' is a call to render personal and practical assistance to the Jewish people.

'Through the mercy shown you,' said the Apostle Paul, *'they also may obtain mercy'* (Romans 11:31). With few exceptions, the Church has not been noted for extending mercy to the Jewish people. In many cases, the wrath of man has worked unrighteousness – with tragic results!

But thank God, it is a new day and the Lord is doing a new thing in the earth. He is calling forth a ministry of mercy from the Church – active mercy which reaches out to feed the hungry, clothe the needy, comfort the afflicted, and deliver the oppressed.

As Christians reach out in the love of Jesus with Holy Spirit-inspired sensitivity and humility, wonderful miracles of healing and reconciliation will take place.

Even now, God is opening tremendous doors of opportunity

all over the world. With the rising tide of anti-semitism, Christians are being afforded a unique chance to support and shelter God's Ancient Covenant People as they seek to return to Israel.

A case in point is the present massive *Aliyah* from the Commonwealth of Independent States. For many years the Spirit of God has been preparing the hearts of believers in Scandinavian and European countries to receive and assist Soviet Jews as they make their way through these regions to Israel.

Prophetic-minded Christians are assisting would-be immigrants with food and medicine, clothing and accommodation, Russian Bibles and literature about Israel. Courageous believers are risking their lives to transport Jews from the war-torn regions of Moldova and Trans-Dniester to Odessa, where they can connect with flights to Israel.

Other visionaries are sponsoring ocean liner voyages for new immigrants from the Black Sea port of Odessa to the Israeli port of Haifa. Over the past four years, Christians representing various nations and organizations have sponsored more than fifty planeloads of Soviet immigrants.

But getting the new immigrants to Israel is only the beginning of the story. Christians are also involved in the huge task of absorption: the distribution of clothing, personal effects and household wares, assistance with housing and other financial needs etc.

Every gift that is given, every service that is offered, every task that is joyfully performed, contributes to the comforting of Jerusalem and the building up of Zion.

Indeed, God is not unjust to forget the work and labour of love that we show toward His Name, in our ministry to His 'set apart ones'.

For as the Apostle Paul said in 1 Corinthians 15:58; *'Therefore, my beloved brethren, be firm (steadfast), immovable, always abounding in the work of the Lord – that is, always being superior (excelling, doing more than enough) in the service of the Lord, knowing and being continually aware that your labour in the Lord is not futile – never wasted or to no purpose'* (Amplified).

Law of Reciprocation

In his epistle to the Church at Rome, the Apostle Paul explained the 'Law of Reciprocation' that governs the relationship between Christians and Jews:

> *'But now I am going to Jerusalem to minister to the saints. For it pleased those from Macedonia and Achaia to make a certain contribution for the poor among the saints who are in Jerusalem. It pleased them indeed, and they are their debtors. For if the Gentiles have been partakers of their spiritual things, their duty is also to minister to them in material things.'* (Romans 15:25–27)

As Gentile Christians, we are partakers of the Jews' *spiritual things*. Through Israel has come the Law and the Prophets, the Covenants and the Scriptures, Apostles and Teachers, and most important of all, Messiah Yeshua, Blessed be His Name!

We, who were without Messiah, being aliens from the Commonwealth of Israel and strangers from the covenants of promise, having no hope and without God in the world, have been brought near by the Blood of Messiah, and are now fellow citizens with the saints and members of the household of God!

What shall we then render to the House of Israel for all the benefits God has bestowed on us through them?

Chapter 13

All Israel Will Be Saved

'...hardening in part has happened to Israel until the fulness of the Gentiles has come in. And so all Israel will be saved...'
(Romans 11:25–26)

The consummation of God's dealings with Israel is described in five simple and glorious words: *All Israel will be saved!*

This statement immediately throws a proverbial spanner into the theological works of some Christians. What does *'all Israel'* mean? Will every Jew on the face of the earth be saved? When will the fulness of the Gentiles come in? Does *'the fulness of the Gentiles'* mean the rapture of the Church? If so, does this mean that God will not deal redemptively with Israel until after the return of Messiah Jesus?

Whilst we do not have the answer to every prophetic question, we do have a *'sure word of prophecy'* in the Holy Scriptures, that shines as a light in a dark place (2 Peter 1:19).

May God help us to avoid the peril of neglecting biblical prophecy and ignoring the signs of the times. Spiritual ignorance results in confusion and deception. God said, *'My people have gone into captivity because they have no knowledge'* (Isaiah 5:13).

May God also help us to avoid the peril of religious dogmatism when it comes to interpreting biblical prophecy. At present, we are seeing in a mirror, dimly. Hindsight always has 20/20 vision!

'All Israel'

'All Israel' refers to the remnant of Jewish people who are appointed unto salvation, both Old Covenant saints and New Covenant believers in *Yeshua HaMashiach*.

Arguing the case of grace and faith with the churches in Galatia, the Apostle Paul said, *'only those who are of faith are sons of Abraham'* (Galatians 3:7). And in his letter to the Church at Rome, Paul asserted that a true or completed Jew is one whose heart is right with God, being justified by faith through grace.

Moreover, true circumcision is of the heart and is accomplished by the power of the Holy Spirit, not the letter of the law (Romans 2:28–29; 4:1–25).

Thus, the 'Israel of God' or the true and complete Israel consists of Jews who believe in the Lord and Messiah Jesus (Galatians 6:16). Those who are born Jews, not only through a natural birth of flesh and blood, but more importantly, through a spiritual birth of faith and obedience (John 1:13; 3:5).

There is no basis in the Word of God for believing that every Jewish person on earth, or even in *Eretz* Israel, will be saved. God's ways do not change, and throughout history He has always saved a **remnant** from destruction. The word 'remnant' does not necessarily indicate a tiny minority; rather, it demonstrates that God calls forth a people for His Name *out of* the nations, and of Israel itself.

The faith of the Apostle Paul did not extend beyond the saving of a remnant of Israel: *'Even so then, at this present time there is a remnant according to the election of grace,'* and *'if by any means I may provoke to jealousy those who are my flesh and save some of them'* (Romans 11:5, 14).

It should be stated, however, that the 'remnant' of Israel represents a glorious harvest of souls for the Kingdom of God, the magnitude and magnificence of which is beyond our comprehension!

The Fulness of the Gentiles

What does the phrase, *'the fulness of the Gentiles'* mean? It is wrong and presumptuous to equate the fulness of the Gentiles with the rapture of the Church. Rather, *'the fulness of the Gentiles'* signifies the consummation of God's purposes in the nations.

'The fulness of the Gentiles coming in' indicates the completion of that which began with the household of Cornelius, the Roman Centurion: God visiting the nations to take out of them a people for His Name.

This does not mean, however, that the last Gentile has to be saved before the veil can be removed from the hearts of the Jewish people. On the contrary, the completion of God's redemptive purposes in the nations and the spiritual restoration of Israel is a continuum; two inseparable events which interact. One cannot take place without the other!

The outpouring of the Holy Spirit began on the Day of Pentecost in the city of Jerusalem, with one hundred and twenty Jewish believers. It quickly spread to Judea and Samaria, and within a few years to the nations of the world.

The circle of redemption is almost complete. What began in Jerusalem will also end in Jerusalem. There will be another 'Jerusalem Pentecost' at the end of the age. Once again, the glory of the Lord will be revealed in Zion and the Spirit of Grace and Supplication will be poured out on the inhabitants of Jerusalem!

Looking through the telescope of the Spirit, Zechariah envisioned the full circle of redemption and spoke of the terminus of God's dealings. Although the prophecy bears immediate reference to post-exilic Jerusalem in the time of Zerubbabel, the scope of the language would indicate a future Messianic era.

> *'Thus says the LORD of hosts: "I am zealous for Jerusalem and for Zion with great zeal ... I am returning to Jerusalem with mercy; My house shall be built in it," says the LORD of hosts, "And a surveyor's line shall be stretched out over Jerusalem ... the LORD will again comfort Zion, and will again choose Jerusalem ... Jerusalem shall be inhabited as*

> towns without walls, because of the multitude of men and
> livestock in it. For I," says the LORD, "will be a wall of fire
> all around her, and I will be the glory in her midst ... Sing
> and rejoice, O daughter of Zion! For behold, I am coming
> and I will dwell in your midst," says the LORD.'
> (Zechariah 1:14, 16, 17; 2:4, 5, 10)

Twentieth Century believers are witnesses of God's zeal for
Jerusalem and Zion. Before our very eyes, God is returning to
Jerusalem with mercy. He is once again comforting Zion and
choosing Jerusalem.

But in our ebullience, we must not lose sight of the Divine
purpose of restoration. God is returning to Jerusalem with one
thought in mind: *To build His house in the midst of the city ... to
dwell among His people ... to reveal the fire of His holiness and
the glory of His majesty!*

Moreover, Zechariah associates the building of the house of
the Lord in Jerusalem with a worldwide movement of God's
Spirit, resulting in the evangelization of *many nations*:

> 'Many nations shall be joined to the LORD in that day, and
> they shall become My people. And I will dwell in your
> midst. Then you will know that the LORD of hosts has sent
> Me to you. And the LORD will take possession of Judah as
> His inheritance in the Holy Land, and will again choose
> Jerusalem.' (Zechariah 2:11–12)

Many scholars believe that the spokesman in this passage is
Messiah Jesus – the 'Sent One' of the Lord of hosts. The Word
of God declares that 'in that day' – in the day that the Lord
builds His house in Jerusalem and moves with revival power
among the nations – the people of Israel will know that Jesus is
the 'Sent One' and Messiah of Whom the prophets spoke!

The veil will be removed and Jesus' prayer will be answered,
'that the world (including Israel) *may believe and know that You
have sent Me'* (John 17:21, 23).

The Rebuilt Temple

The question of the rebuilding of the temple is one of the hottest potatoes on the Bible prophecy grill. Some commentators believe that a Third Temple will actually be built on the site of the First and Second Temples in the Old City of Jerusalem. However, such a proposition is fraught with difficulty due to the fact that the Temple Mount area is under Arab control, and moreover, is regarded as the third most holy shrine of Islam.

Dr Asher Kaufman, a noted professor of physics at Hebrew University, spent sixteen years investigating the exact location of the Second Temple. According to Dr Kaufman's painstaking research, the Second Temple was situated north of the present **Dome of the Rock**, with a clearance of twenty-six metres at its nearest point.

Hence, it is technically possible to build the Jewish temple without dismantling the Moslem Dome of the Rock. But even if religious Jews were willing to accept such a compromise (which I very much doubt), devout Moslems could never acquiesce to such a visible display of co-existence on such a sacred piece of territory.

Of course, it is well within the ability of God to supernaturally resolve this problem and to clear the way for a temple or anything else that might be on His agenda.

However, the real question concerns the nature of the rebuilt temple: Is it natural or is it spiritual?

> '*You also, as living stones, are being built up a spiritual house, a holy priesthood, to offer up spiritual sacrifices acceptable to God through Jesus Christ.*' (1 Peter 2:5)

That which was natural and temporal under the Mosaic Covenant is spiritual and eternal under the New Covenant.

Under the Mosaic Covenant there was a natural tabernacle (and later a temple) and a natural priesthood, which offered up natural sacrifices. But under the New Covenant there is a spiritual temple (the local Body of Messiah), and a spiritual priesthood (comprising all believers), which offers up spiritual sacrifices (prayer, praise, worship etc.)

When Jesus died on the Cross, the veil of the temple was torn in two from top to bottom (Matthew 27:51). The fact that it was torn *from top to bottom* signifies that it was an act of God, not man.

Jesus had previously warned that the temple would be left desolate (Matthew 23:38). The veil was torn as the Spirit of God departed from the Holy of Holies. But fifty days after the death of Jesus, *when the Day of Pentecost had fully come*, the Spirit of God took up residence in a new temple – the hearts and lives of 120 Jewish believers gathered in an upper room in Jerusalem!

Filled with the Holy Spirit, this new kind of priesthood began to offer up a new kind of sacrifice: *'they all began to speak with other tongues ... the wonderful works of God ... as the Spirit gave them utterance'* (Acts 2:4, 11).

The outpouring of the Holy Spirit on the Day of Pentecost marked the inauguration of a New Covenant between God and man – a whole new order of relationship made possible by the death and resurrection of Jesus.

Under the Mosaic Covenant God was *with* His people, but under the New Covenant God is *in* His people (John 14:17). The Kingdom of God is in their midst, even in their very hearts (Luke 17:21). Their bodies are temples of the Holy Spirit, and upon their gathering together they form one great temple, a dwelling place of God by His Spirit (1 Corinthians 6:19; Ephesians 2:21, 22).

The question is, having left the natural, material temple to take up residence in a spiritual temple, and having instituted a new order of ministry based on spiritual realities, will God ever go back to a physical temple and a Levitical priesthood that offers up animal sacrifices?

The answer, in my view, is unequivocally NO! I would go so far as to say that if the Jews do succeed in building a temple in Jerusalem, God will have no part in it. The notion that after accepting the sacrifice of the Blood of His own Son, God might once again accept the sacrifice of bulls and goats, and even dwell in a temple where such sacrifices are being made, is nothing short of blasphemous.

And to this I would add the words of the Apostle Paul at the Areopagus:

> *'God, who made the world and everything in it, since He is Lord of heaven and earth, does not dwell in temples made with hands. Nor is He worshipped with men's hands, as though He needed anything, since He gives to all life, breath, and all things.'* (Acts 17:24–25)

A Temple Made Without Hands

Some believers are more interested in the prospect of a stone temple than in the reality of an indigenous Israeli Church.

My good friend, Kelvin Crombie, guide and historian of Christ Church, Jerusalem, the first Protestant church in the Middle East, told me that he often fields questions from visiting tour groups about the building of the Third Temple. Kelvin usually responds by saying, 'Well, if you come here next Shabbat, you will see the Temple that the Lord is building – Jews and Gentiles worshipping together in one Body of Messiah.' But some people just aren't interested in the organism of a living fellowship – they are too obsessed with the romantic ideal of a physical building.

The Lord Jesus is building His Church – the spiritual temple – in Jerusalem, as well as in Tel Aviv, Haifa, Ashkelon, Tiberias, and in towns and cities throughout the Land. This is the temple which we, as Christians, should be most interested in and supportive of.

It grieves my heart to see Christians collecting money for a Third Temple and offering to assist in its construction. A rebuilt temple would be the antithesis of the Body of Messiah, and hence, a perfect platform for the Antichrist and his counterfeit religion.

God is concerned about the integrity of the Land. In fact, I was praying on one occasion about the possible repartitioning of Israel, and the Lord said to me, 'I am more concerned about the Land than you are!'

God's concern for the Land notwithstanding, His main

priority for Israel and the nations is: *'I will pour out My Spirit on all flesh!'* (Joel 2:28).

As New Covenant believers, we must be sure to identify first and foremost with the spiritual priorities of God's Kingdom. This does not preclude *Christian Zionism* – Christian support for the right of Jews to return to and build up their ancient homeland – but it does rule out Christian support for a rebuilt temple and a reinstated Levitical priesthood, which are incompatible with New Covenant realities.

Ezekiel's Vision

Ezekiel was a young priest, probably from the Zadokite family, who was deported to Babylon during the second siege of Jerusalem in 597 BC. About four years later, Ezekiel's life was dramatically and permanently changed by a vision of the majesty of God and the four Living Creatures that surround His Throne.

> *'...As I was among the captives by the River Chebar, that the heavens were opened and I saw visions of God ... a whirlwind was coming out of the north, a great cloud with raging fire engulfing itself; and brightness was all around it and radiating out of its midst like the color of amber, out of the midst of the fire. Also from within it came the likeness of four living creatures ... And above the firmament over their heads was the likeness of a throne, in appearance like a sapphire stone; on the likeness of the throne was a likeness with the appearance of a man high above it. Also from the appearance of His waist and upward I saw, as it were, the color of amber with the appearance of fire all around within it; and from the appearance of His waist and downward I saw, as it were, the appearance of fire with brightness all around. Like the appearance of a rainbow in a cloud on a rainy day, so was the appearance of the brightness all around it. This was the likeness of the glory of the LORD...'*
> (Ezekiel 1:1–28)

The central theme of Ezekiel's prophecy, and indeed, the

consuming passion of his life, is the *glory* and *presence* of God in the midst of His people. Significantly, the prophecy closes with a vision of a glorified city whose name is *Yahweh Shammah*, **'The Lord is there.'**

But in between the opening stanzas of God's visitation and the final testimony of God's abiding Presence, there is a tragic saga of idolatry, apostasy, captivity and desolation.

In chapter eight, Ezekiel is transported in spirit to Jerusalem where he observes the idolatry and abominations taking place in the temple of God. God is holy and jealous, and will not share His worship with any other creature or object. The temple of God is dedicated to the exclusive residence of the Holy Spirit. Thus, if idolatry is tolerated in the temple, it is only a matter of time before God removes His Presence and leaves the house spiritually desolate.

In chapter ten, Ezekiel watches mournfully as the glory of the Lord departs from the temple. God is literally being driven out of His own house! However, the Presence of God does not depart in one movement, but slowly, almost reluctantly. First to the threshold, then over the cherubim, then to the east gate, and finally to the Mount of Olives, east of the city.

The next thirteen chapters record the story of a *departed glory*, a *desolate temple*, and a *dispersed people*. Immanuel, God with us, is our *raison d'etre* – the very purpose of our existence. When the Presence of God departs, the canopy of protection is removed, resulting in impoverishment and enslavement.

But chapters thirty-four through forty are a magnificent testimony to God's grace, detailing the restoration of the people to the Land, and upon returning to the Land, the restoration of the people to the Lord.

Chapters forty through forty-eight describe the rebuilding of the temple and the restoration of the glory of the Lord. Notice that in restoration, the process is reversed: The *people* are regathered, the *temple* is rebuilt, and then the *glory* returns!

The *Shekinah* of God was the first thing to leave, and will be the last thing to return. But right now, God is preparing a temple fit for His habitation, and into that Living Body of Messiah He will pour the fulness of Him who fills all things everywhere with Himself! (Ephesians 1:23; 2:21–22).

Suddenly He Comes

One of the striking characteristics of the Scriptural Record is the 'sudden work' of the Spirit of God.

God always works according to a pattern, and that pattern is one of long and thorough preparation, and when the appointed time comes, swift and sudden consummation.

Thus, it is instructive to note the 'suddenly's' of Scripture. Speaking of the cleansing of the temple and the restoration of Davidic praise and worship, 2 Chronicles 29:36 says, *'Then Hezekiah and all the people rejoiced that God had prepared the people, since the events took place so suddenly.'*

Speaking of both the first and second advents of Messiah, and in a sense, every intervening visitation of the Holy Spirit, Malachi 3:1 says, *'Behold, I send My messenger, and he will prepare the way before Me. And the LORD, whom you seek, will suddenly come to His temple, even the Messenger of the Covenant, in whom you delight...'*

Speaking of the outpouring of the Holy Spirit at the commencement of the Church age, Acts 2:1–2 says, *'When the Day of Pentecost had fully come, they were all with one accord in one place. And suddenly there came a sound from heaven, as of a rushing mighty wind, and it filled the whole house where they were sitting.'*

God has set Himself to do a quick work in Israel that will boggle the mind of even the most optimistic believer.

Ezekiel describes it as the *Breath of God* coming into a resurrected nation (Ezekiel 37). Other prophets describe it as *rain from heaven*.

In the winter of 1991–92 God demonstrated His great power in the natural realm by sending the heaviest rains in 140 years of recorded history! Several years of semi-drought conditions (coupled with poor water management) had resulted in Israel's main water reservoir, the Sea of Galilee, falling four metres below the full mark, dangerously close to the red line – the lowest point before permanent damage occurred to the ecological makeup of the country's only natural lake. Furthermore, Israel's two main natural underground water aquifers were also severely depleted. Israeli scientists had predicted that it would take several years of good rainfall to restore the country's water resources.

But God had other ideas! By the middle of February, Ashkelon had received over twice its annual average rainfall, Jerusalem and Tel Aviv over 170%, and Haifa and Tiberias around 140%. So much snow had fallen on Mount Hermon that measurements were no longer being taken! Jerusalem was blanketed by snow, and for the first time in 40 years, snow fell in Haifa, Beit Shean, and other low-lying northern cities.

In Rehovot, 92.5mm of rain fell in one 24 hour period – 20% of a year's average rainfall! Heavy flooding occurred in many parts of the country, forcing hundreds of families out of their homes.

In just 3 months, so much water had flowed into the Sea of Galilee that the flood gates at the Southern end of the lake were flung wide open, sending torrents of water rushing down the Jordan River to the Dead Sea.

One reporter called it 'The winter the skies fell in.' It was totally unexpected, unprecedented, and unstoppable!

In the eyes of many believers, it is a case of *'first the natural, then the spiritual'* (1 Corinthians 15:46). The work of God in the natural – an open heaven and an abundance of rain – is a precursor to the work of God in the spiritual – the outpouring of His Spirit on all flesh.

Parallels can easily be drawn between the natural deluge of 1992 and the imminent spiritual deluge of which the Scriptures speak.

First of all, *the rain was universal and non-discriminatory*. It fell throughout the whole Land on the just and the unjust, religious and non-religious, Jews and Arabs, Christians and Moslems. In like manner, God promises to pour out His Spirit on *all flesh*, to gather in a harvest of souls from every nation, tribe, people, and tongue, to break down the wall of separation between them, and to make them into one Body of Messiah.

Secondly, *the rain was a manifestation of God's sovereign power, and could not be controlled or stopped by any human agency*. Likewise, the outpouring of the Spirit will be the work of God and not man, and any attempt to halt it will be like trying to restrain Niagara Falls with a teaspoon!

Thirdly, *the rain disrupted the lifestyle of many communities*. The early Church 'turned the world upside down' with their message. Great cities were stirred to uproar by the working of the Spirit of God. Yet once more Jerusalem will be filled with the teaching of Messiah and the demonstration of the power of God.

Fourthly, *the rain accomplished in months, what men predicted would take years*. Like the disciples of old, we may be struggling to make headway on the stormy sea, but when Jesus gets into the boat, we will be suddenly transported to the other side! (John 6:21). God is able to accomplish more in five months than we could accomplish in fifty years!

Indeed, *'He will finish the work and cut it short in righteousness, because the LORD will make a short work upon the earth'* (Romans 9:28).

Blessed Is He Who Comes

During His last week of ministry in Jerusalem, the Lord Jesus made some very important prophetic statements about the destiny of Israel. Reading them, one can sense the pathos of immediate grief and ultimate hope that must have pervaded the Saviour's heart.

> *'O Jerusalem, Jerusalem, the one who kills the prophets and stones those who are sent to her! How often I wanted to gather your children together, as a hen gathers her chicks under her wings, but you were not willing! See! Your house is left to you desolate; for I say to you, you shall see Me no more till you say, "Blessed is He who comes in the Name of the LORD!"'* (Matthew 23:37–39)

Within days of Jesus' prophecy, the house of the Lord was empty. *Ichabod*. The Spirit of Glory had departed. And some 40 years later, the house itself was reduced to rubble by the Roman Tenth Legion.

But peering down the corridor of time, Jesus saw another generation; one which given the chance, would respond to Him in faith and love.

The utterance *'Blessed is He who comes in the Name of the Lord'* forms part of the Egyptian Hallel (Psalm 113 through Psalm 118), and was traditionally chanted by worshippers at each of the major feasts of Israel. The language is clearly Messianic, and embodies the age-old expectation of a Deliverer-King who would sit on the throne of David and judge the nations in righteousness.

People often mis-read the Lord's statement as follows: *'When I return you will see Me, and then you will say, "Blessed is He…"'* But Jesus didn't say, *'When you see Me, you will say…'* He said, *'You will not see Me **until you say**…'* In other words, the 'saying' precedes the 'seeing'.

This last generation of Jews will experience a change of heart with regard to the Person and Work of the Lord Jesus. God will give them a Spirit of wisdom and revelation in the knowledge of the Messiah. The eyes of their understanding will be flooded with light.

As a result, they will start acclaiming *Yeshua* as King-Messiah, the Son of David and the Hope of Israel. They will begin to say of Jesus, *'Blessed is He who comes in the Name of the Lord.'*

And when significant numbers of Jews start acknowledging Jesus as Lord and Messiah, it is a sure sign that His return is near.

Life from the Dead

What effect will the spiritual restoration of Israel have on the Church? The Apostle Paul answers that question in Romans chapter eleven:

> *'Now if their fall is riches for the world, and their failure riches for the Gentiles, how much more their fullness? For if their being cast away is the reconciling of the world, what will their acceptance be but life from the dead?'*
>
> (Romans 11:12, 15)

The reconciliation of the Jewish people to the Messiah will

bring incalculable blessing to the whole redeemed community. It will release new streams of power and authority in the Church, and a tidal wave of resurrection life that will sweep the whole earth. It will both precipitate and consummate the greatest ingathering of souls that the Church has ever known.

To this I would add a portion of the prophetic Word delivered by Lance Lambert at Mount Carmel in 1986:

'And in the midst of nations on earth seething with unrest and conflict, I have set My Israel. Yes, I say "My Israel", even though they walk in disobedience and transgression in the stubbornness of their hearts, divorced from Me through unbelief. Nevertheless, always remember that I made them enemies of the Gospel for your sake. I, the Lord, I Myself blinded them and hardened them that salvation might come to the Gentiles in fulness. Yet they are still Mine, beloved of Me, with a tender and an undying love. They are My kith and kin and I love them.

Shall I give them up for all that they have done to Me, says the Lord? Yet I have surrendered them to sorrow, to anguish of heart and to continuous suffering. But I have never given them up. In all their affliction I was afflicted, though I neither delivered nor saved them from death. Nevertheless, I have been present. I, the King of Israel, have been present, although unnoticed and unregarded, in all their sufferings. There was no gas chamber, no massacre in which I was not present; but now the time has surely come when I shall receive them, for I will reveal Myself to them and with astonishment they will recognize Me.

For in the midst of these judgments, multitudes upon multitudes will be saved from the nations. You will hardly know how to bring the harvest in, but My Spirit will equip you for the task. And to Israel I will also turn in that day, and I will melt the hardening which has befallen her. I will turn her blindness into clear sight, and tear away the veil on her heart. Then shall she be redeemed with heart-bursting joy, and will become a fountain of new and resurrection life to the whole company of the redeemed.'[1]

I would also like to draw once more on the prophetic observations of Rick Joyner in his book, *The Harvest*.

> 'For almost two milleniums God's purposes were centralized in His dealings with the Jews. Then for almost two milleniums His purpose was concentrated with the Church, which is spiritual Israel or those who are Jews according to the heart (Romans 2:29). At the end of the age there is to be a joining of the two into one, through Jesus, in such a way that it will be the crowning glory of the Lord's entire testimony of redemption.
>
> This is the grafting back in of the "natural branches" of which Paul prophesied in his letter to the Romans. As he so accurately foresaw, if the rejection of the Jews resulted in reconciliation for the world, then their reacceptance will actually bring life from the dead, or the beginning of the resurrection (Romans 11:15). Through this union of Israel and the Church, in Jesus, there will be a release of life and power unequalled on earth since the Spirit first moved on the formless void.'[2]

The Jewish Factor in Revival

There is a definite connection between the fulfilment of God's purposes in Israel, and the breaking forth of revival in the Church.

In chapter two we noted that the 'Evangelical Revival' in 19th century England gave birth to numerous Gospel Societies and missionary endeavours, and coincided with the establishment of the **London Society for Promoting Christianity amongst the Jews**, which was in the vanguard of the movement to create a Jewish national homeland in *Eretz* Israel.

We find another example of the link between Israel and the Church, or what may be termed, the 'Jewish factor in revival,' in the ministry of the Scottish Presbyterian preacher **Robert Murray M'Cheyne**.

Motivated by a belief that the Gospel should be preached to the Jew first, M'Cheyne went on a preaching mission to Palestine in 1839.

A short time later, revival broke out in the Scottish city of Kilsyth through the preaching of William Burns. Although there were various contributing factors such as prayer, fasting, and a powerful preaching of the Cross, M'Cheyne and his colleagues felt that there was a definite link between the Scottish revival and the Jewish mission to Palestine.

M'Cheyne believed that if the Church would discharge its ministry to the Jews, revival would follow among the Gentiles, and that such a sequence would not be an isolated phenomenon, but a lasting pattern, for the salvation of the Jewish people meant the restoration of the Church.

Furthermore, M'Cheyne believed that **if we would be evangelistic as God would have us to be, and not only dispense the light on every hand, but dispense it first to the Jew, then we would see the same outpouring in our day and in our land that he had witnessed in Kilsyth in 1839![3]**

In recent years, a number of Eastern European and Latin American countries have granted their resident Jewish populations freedom to emigrate to Israel. The remarkable fact is that almost every nation which has obeyed God's injunction to 'Let My people go,' has been blessed with a mighty outpouring of the Holy Spirit, whereas the nations which have refused to let the Jews go continue to languish in spiritual poverty!

There is no doubt but that the 'Jewish factor' is destined to play a significant part in the last great revival before the return of the Lord.

The Anointing of the King

King David was both a natural ancestor and a prophetic type of the Lord Jesus. The anointing of David as king over all Israel anticipates the instalment of a Greater King in Zion.

> *'Then all the tribes of Israel came to David at Hebron and spoke, saying, "Indeed we are your bone and flesh. Also, in time past, when Saul was king over us, you were the one who led Israel out and brought them in; and the LORD said to you, 'You shall shepherd My people Israel, and be ruler*

over Israel.'" Therefore all the elders of Israel came to the king at Hebron, and King David made a covenant with them at Hebron before the LORD. And they anointed David king over Israel.' (2 Samuel 5:1–3)

God the Father has already installed Messiah Jesus as King on His holy hill of Zion (Psalm 2:6). It is only a matter of time before that which is established in the heavenly Zion is also established in the earthly Zion. Yesterday, today and forever, Jesus is the King of the Jews!

The word 'Hebron' means 'seat of association or place of covenant'. The Holy Spirit is going to lead Jesus' brethren after the flesh, the Jewish people, into a place of covenant relationship with their Redeemer-King.

Ever since the chief priests cried, *'Not this Man, but Barabbas'*, and *'We have no king but Caesar'*, the Jewish nation has been ruled by the 'house of Saul'. King Saul was a man of the flesh – carnal, selfish and avaricious. As such, he epitomises the weakness of human government.

David was a man of the Spirit with a disposition to do the will of God. As such, he represents the King who reigns in righteousness and rules with justice – the Good Shepherd who gives His life for the sheep.

Israel will come to recognize *Yeshua* as the One of whom the prophets spoke. Looking upon Him with eyes of tender love, they will say, *'The Lord said to you, "You shall shepherd My people Israel, and be ruler over Israel."'*

And with the praises of their mouths and the worship of their hearts, they will anoint Him *King of the Jews!*

The Lord's brethren after the flesh will be the last to 'bring back the King' (2 Samuel 19:11, 12). The nation of Israel holds one of the keys to Jesus' Second Coming. Their acclamation of His Kingship will be the crowning glory of world revival, and better still, will prepare the way for His triumphant return!

*If their fall is riches for the world, and their failure riches for the Gentiles, how much more their fulness! Indeed, **how much more!***

References

1. *He will tell you things to come*. Derek Prince Ministries, PO Box 300, Fort Lauderdale, Florida, 33302, USA.
2. *The Harvest*, by Rick Joyner. Morningstar Publications, Pineville, NC, p. 132.
3. *Memoir and Remains of Robert Murray M'Cheyne*, by Andrew Bonar. Banner of Truth, Carlisle, PA.

Chapter 14

One New Man

'For He Himself is our peace, who has made both one, and has broken down the middle wall of separation, having abolished in His flesh the enmity, that is the law of commandments contained in ordinances, so as to create in Himself one new man from the two, thus making peace.'

(Ephesians 2:14–15)

The hope of the Middle East is not a 'New World Order,' but rather, 'One New Man.' There is no durable or comprehensive solution to the problems of the Middle East apart from Messiah Jesus and His spiritual Kingdom of righteousness, peace and joy.

The catchcry of the world is 'peace, peace', but fallen man is incapable of living in peace with his neighbour unless he experiences a radical change of heart. For this reason, the pseudo-peace that the world clamours for and occasionally obtains (which, at best, is merely a cessation of hostilities), is doomed to end in *'sudden destruction'* (1 Thessalonians 5:3).

Man cannot make peace with man. It requires the intercession of a Higher Power, the Lord God Himself, to bring true and lasting peace on earth.

'For unto us a Child is born, unto us a Son is given; and the government will be upon His shoulder. And His Name will be called Wonderful, Counsellor, Mighty God, Everlasting Father, Prince of Peace. Of the increase of His government

and peace there will be no end, upon the throne of David and over His kingdom, to order it and establish it with judgment and justice from that time forward, even forever. The zeal of the LORD of hosts will perform this.'

(Isaiah 9:6–7)

The Child-Son of whom the prophet speaks is *Yeshua HaMashiach* – Immanuel, God with us in human form. He alone is perfectly fit to govern; He alone is utterly faithful and true; He alone judges with absolute righteousness and equity.

One of Messiah's best-loved titles is *'Prince of Peace'*. But do we understand what it really means: *that it is Messiah's rule which brings peace!* Peace is an attribute of God's Kingdom and thus, can only be enjoyed under Messiah's government.

In Psalm 122:6 we are instructed to *'pray for the peace of Jerusalem.'* However, true peace will not come to this or any other region of the world until Messiah is enthroned in Jerusalem.

Does this mean that we should resign ourselves to conflict and strife, hoping and praying for the soon return of the Lord? Or has God provided an alternative forum for peace – one which transcends politics, culture, ethnicity, territorialism etc.

The New Ethnos

The born-again, Spirit-filled Church of Messiah is the 'New Ethnos,' God's holy nation, in which there is neither Jew nor Greek, circumcised nor uncircumcised, male nor female, slave nor free – only a new creation in Messiah Jesus!

Consider the Apostolic testimony:

'You have put on the new man who is renewed in knowledge according to the image of Him who created him, where there is neither Greek nor Jew, circumcised nor uncircumcised, barbarian, Scythian, slave nor free, but Christ is all and in all.' (Colossians 3:10–11)

208

> *'For you are all sons of God through faith in Christ Jesus. For as many of you as were baptized into Christ have put on Christ. There is neither Jew nor Greek, there is neither slave nor free, there is neither male nor female; for you are all one in Christ Jesus.'*
> (Galatians 3:26–28)

When one is born again of the Spirit and baptized into the Body of Messiah, one does not lose his or her personal identity, national heritage, or cultural distinction; rather, one assumes a **superior identity** as a new creature in Messiah.

The spiritual must always take precedence over the natural. Thus, *'I am firstly a follower of Jesus, and secondly a Jew,'* or *'firstly a follower of Jesus, and secondly an Arab,'* etc. My spiritual and eternal identity in Messiah transcends my natural and temporal identity on earth.

When we allow our natural birth and all that it signifies to take precedence over our spiritual birth, we frustrate the grace of God and negate the reality of being *'in Messiah'*.

One of the enemy's most successful ploys is to get us to focus on our natural differences, rather than on our spiritual commonality.

Whether we are Jew, Arab, British, Indian, or German, there is no greater calling than to be a son of God through faith in Messiah Jesus! There is no greater privilege than to be 'in Messiah' – a member of His Body, a citizen of His eternal city, a subject of His glorious Kingdom, a living stone in His spiritual house!

Even though the Apostle Paul was *'circumcised the eighth day, of the stock of Israel, of the tribe of Benjamin, a Hebrew of the Hebrews, and a Pharisee who scrupulously observed the Law,'* he counted all this as loss compared with the priceless privilege, the overwhelming preciousness, and the surpassing value of knowing Messiah Jesus, and being found *in Him* (Philippians 3:4–9).

Being *'in Messiah'* was the supreme reality of Paul's life. Expressions like 'in Messiah,' 'in Him,' 'in Whom,' 'through Whom,' etc., appear approximately 140 times in the New Testament, mostly in Paul's letters to the churches.

If the reality of the New Creation can grip our hearts, it will lift us above all political strife, racial tension, and territorial conflict. Jesus Himself is our peace. He has broken down the middle wall of separation. We are one *in Him!*

A Mystery Revealed

The Apostle Paul speaks of the merging of Jews and Gentiles into one Body of Messiah as a 'mystery revealed':

> *'How that by revelation He made known to me the mystery ... which in other ages was not made known to the sons of men, as it has now been revealed by the Spirit to His holy apostles and prophets: That the Gentiles should be fellow heirs, of the same body, and partakers of His promise in Christ through the Gospel.'* (Ephesians 3:3a, 5–6)

God intends for the Body of Messiah to be a model of love and unity to a strife-torn world. Jesus said, *'By this all will know that you are My disciples, if you have love for one another'* (John 13:35). And before His death He prayed *'that they all may be one in Us, that the world may believe that You sent Me'* (John 17:21).

Moreover, the unity of Messiah's Body is a testimony to the principalities and powers in heavenly places that seek to exploit our cultural diversity: *'To the intent that now the manifold wisdom of God might be made known by the Church to the principalities and powers in the heavenly places, according to the eternal purpose which He accomplished in Christ Jesus our Lord'* (Ephesians 3:10, 11).

It is a declaration of the power of God's love – that the goodness of God is greater than evil; that mercy and grace triumph over hatred and malice!

The only hope for true peace in the Middle East in this present era lies in the Body of Messiah. Therefore, to *'pray for the peace of Jerusalem'* is to pray for the building up of Messiah's Body – the only sphere in which true peace can be achieved!

Shepherds After God's Heart

The Gospel of Matthew, chapter nine, tells how Jesus went about the cities and villages of Galilee, teaching in the synagogues, preaching the Gospel of the Kingdom, and healing every sickness and every disease among the people.

> *'But when He saw the multitudes, He was moved with compassion for them, because they were weary and scattered, like sheep having no shepherd. Then He said to His disciples, "The harvest truly is plentiful, but the labourers are few. Therefore pray the Lord of the harvest to send out labourers into His harvest."'*   (Matthew 9:36–38)

The prophet Isaiah described the human family as a flock of sheep that has gone astray, every one having turned to his own way (Isaiah 53:6).

Therefore, we are to ask the Lord of the harvest (the Great Shepherd of our souls) to send forth labourers, or more literally, *shepherds* into the harvest field, to find the lost sheep, lead them back to the fold and care for them with His love.

It is highly significant that in three of the major 'Aliyah prophecies' of Jeremiah, God speaks of personally shepherding His people, or of giving them shepherds according to His own heart.

> *'"Return, O backsliding children," says the LORD; "for I am married to you. I will take you, one from a city and two from a family, and I will bring you to Zion. And I will give you shepherds according to My heart, who will feed you with knowledge and understanding."'*   (Jeremiah 3:14–15)

> *'"But I will gather the remnant of My flock out of all countries where I have driven them, and bring them back to their folds; and they shall be fruitful and increase. I will set up shepherds over them who will feed them; and they shall fear no more, nor be dismayed, nor shall they be lacking," says the LORD.'*   (Jeremiah 23:3–4)

> *'"Hear the word of the LORD, O nations, and declare it in the isles afar off, and say, 'He who scattered Israel will gather him, and keep him as a shepherd does his flock.'"'*
>
> (Jeremiah 31:10)

Many Christians are excited about the 'gathering' of the Jewish people, and rightly so, but now is the time to get involved in the 'shepherding' of the house of Israel.

By the grace of God, there are now more than thirty-five Messianic congregations in the Land of Israel, composed of Jews and Gentiles, worshipping the one Lord and Saviour, Jesus the Messiah. The Messianic Body is growing, despite fierce opposition from religious extremists and certain forms of social discrimination.

But it is a relatively young movement, in urgent need of pastors and teachers to feed the various flocks with knowledge and understanding of God's Word. Thank God for the faithful servants who have borne the burden in the heat of the day and have nurtured the fledgling Messianic community.

However, if the Messianic Body is to become what God intends it to be, both quantitatively and qualitatively, there must be a multiplication of ministry, or, to put it another way, a broadening of the shepherding base.

The answer is not found in the importing of pastors and teachers from overseas, but rather, in the raising up of local Israeli leadership.

In the final analysis, the work of God in Israel will stand or fall on the strength of the indigenous Israeli Church. And the indigenous Israel Church will, in turn, stand or fall on the strength of the local leadership.

The Church that Jesus is building in Israel is uniquely Israeli. It is not a colonial outpost of the Church in Great Britain or the United States. And to successfully accomplish God's purposes, it must present an 'Israeli face' to the nation.

That being said, the Messianic Body still needs our prayers, financial support, encouragement, and love.

To all who love Israel, I would say: the Messianic Body represents the best investment of our time, love and money, for more than any other group or organization, it holds the key to the destiny of the nation!

Let me conclude by quoting a portion of an article published exactly one hundred and fifty years ago, entitled, *'Restoration of the Churches of Jerusalem and Judea.'* May it speak with prophetic clarity to our day and generation:

> '. . . the strengthening and fostering of the Jewish Church at Jerusalem is more important, and has more providential signs of its importance, than any other means, perhaps than all other means, now employed for the conversion of Israel. Let it only be matured. It will send forth its own missionaries into every land – men who will penetrate into all countries – surmount all obstacles, and, by bearing upon their front the stamp of nationality, overcome all prejudice of their brethren.'[1]

AMEN!

MAY THEY PROSPER WHO LOVE YOU!

References

1. *Jewish Intelligence*, 1843, pp. 47–48, as quoted in *For the Love of Zion*, by Kelvin Crombie, Hodder & Stoughton, p. 61.

Recommended Reading

The Land and People of Israel

The Uniqueness of Israel by Lance Lambert, Kingsway
Publications.

The Rebirth and Restoration of Israel by Murray Dixon,
Sovereign World.

Battle for Israel by Lance Lambert, Kingsway Publications.

Whose Promised Land? by Murray Dixon, Heinemann
Education.

Understanding Israel by Malcolm Hedding, Sovereign World.

The Last Word on the Middle East by Derek Prince, Chosen
Books.

The Destiny of Israel and the Church by Derek Prince, Word.

Messiah Now! by David Zeidan, Operation Mobilization.

Israel: The Struggle to Survive by David Dolan, Thomas
Nelson.

Land of Promise, Land of Strife by Wesley Pippert, Word.

Pillar of Fire by Yigal Lossin, Shikmona Publishing.

A History of Israel by Rinna Samuel, Weidenfeld & Nicolson.

Jerusalem: The Tragedy & the Triumph by Charles Gulston, Zondervan.

My Life by Golda Meir, Weidenfeld & Nicolson.

Ben-Gurion Prophet of Fire by Dan Kurzman, Simon & Schuster.

If I Forget Thee by Lord Russell of Liverpool, Cassell & Company.

O Jerusalem! by Larry Collins & Dominique Lapierre, Weidenfeld & Nicolson.

A History of Israel: From the Rise of Zionism to Our Time by Howard M. Sachar, Alfred A. Knopf Inc.

Trial and Error by Chaim Weizmann, Harper and Brothers.

Warrior by Ariel Sharon, Simon and Schuster.

Christian Contribution to the Restoration of Israel

For the Love of Zion by Kelvin Crombie, Hodder & Stoughton.

Gideon Goes to War (The story of Wingate) by Leonard Mosley, Arthur Barker Ltd.

The Holocaust and Antisemitism

The Holocaust by Martin Gilbert, Henry Holt.

Our Hands are Stained with Blood by Michael Brown, Destiny-Image.

The Hiding Place by Corrie ten Boom, Hodder & Stoughton.

The Rise and Fall of the Third Reich by William L. Shirer, Simon & Schuster.

The Nazis and the Occult by D. Sklar, Dorset Press.

When Being Jewish Was a Crime by Rachmiel Frydland, Thomas Nelson.

The Anguish of the Jews by Edward Flannery, Macmillan Publishing.

Prayer and Spiritual Warfare

Rees Howells Intercessor by Norman Grubb, Lutterworth Press.

Why Pray for Israel? by Ken Burnett, Kingsway Publications.

Shaping History through Prayer and Fasting by Derek Prince, DPM.

Operation World by Patrick Johnstone, O.M. Publishing.

Aliyah

Let My People Go! by Tom Hess, Progressive Vision.

Exodus II by Steve Lightle, Hunter Books.

Gates of Brass by Jay Rawlings, New Wine Publications.

The Arab People and Islam

The Unholy War by Marius Baar, Thomas Nelson.

The Last of the Giants by George Otis Jnr, Chosen Books.

The Closed Circle by David Pryce-Jones, Paladin.

Jewish History

The Life & Times of Jesus the Messiah by Alfred Edersheim, MacDonald.

Sketches of Jewish Social Life by Alfred Edersheim.

Christ, the Crown of the Torah by Edward Burgess, Zondervan.

Josephus Complete Works, Kregel Publications.

Atlas of Jewish History by Martin Gilbert, Dorset Press.

Historical Fiction

The Zion Chronicles by Bodie Theone, Bethany House.

The Zion Covenant by Bodie Theone, Bethany House.

The Source by James Michener, Fawcett Crest.

Exodus by Leon Uris, Corgi Books.